BIG FISH BETTER BOATS

The History of Sportfishing and Boatbuilding on the Outer Banks

BETHANY BRADSHER

Foreword and interviews by
CHARLES PERRY

Table of Contents

THIS BOOK WAS MADE POSSIBLE BY THE GENEROUS

DONATION OF THE GADDY FAMILY ENDOWMENT

AND THE COOPERATION OF

NORTH CAROLINA WATERMEN UNITED

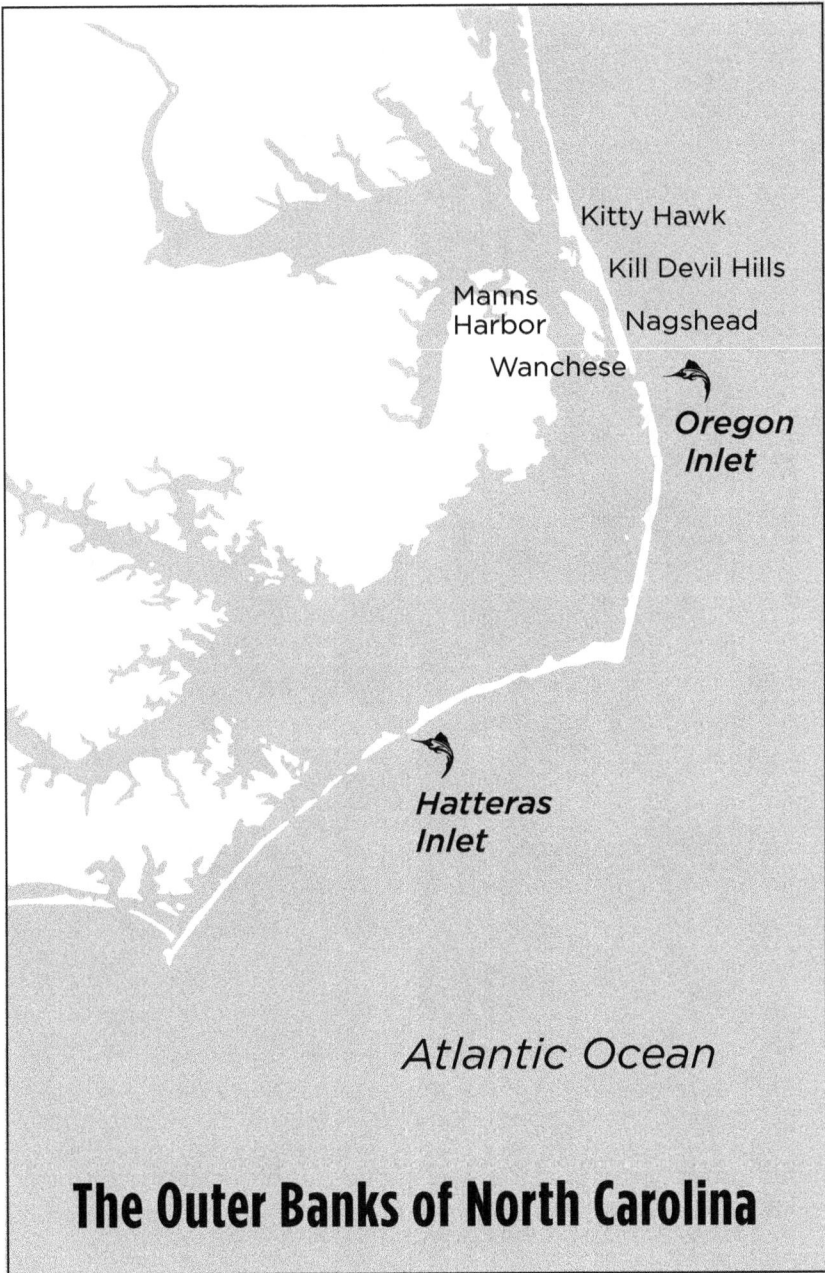

Kitty Hawk

Kill Devil Hills

Manns
Harbor

Nagshead

Wanchese

Oregon
Inlet

Hatteras
Inlet

Atlantic Ocean

The Outer Banks of North Carolina

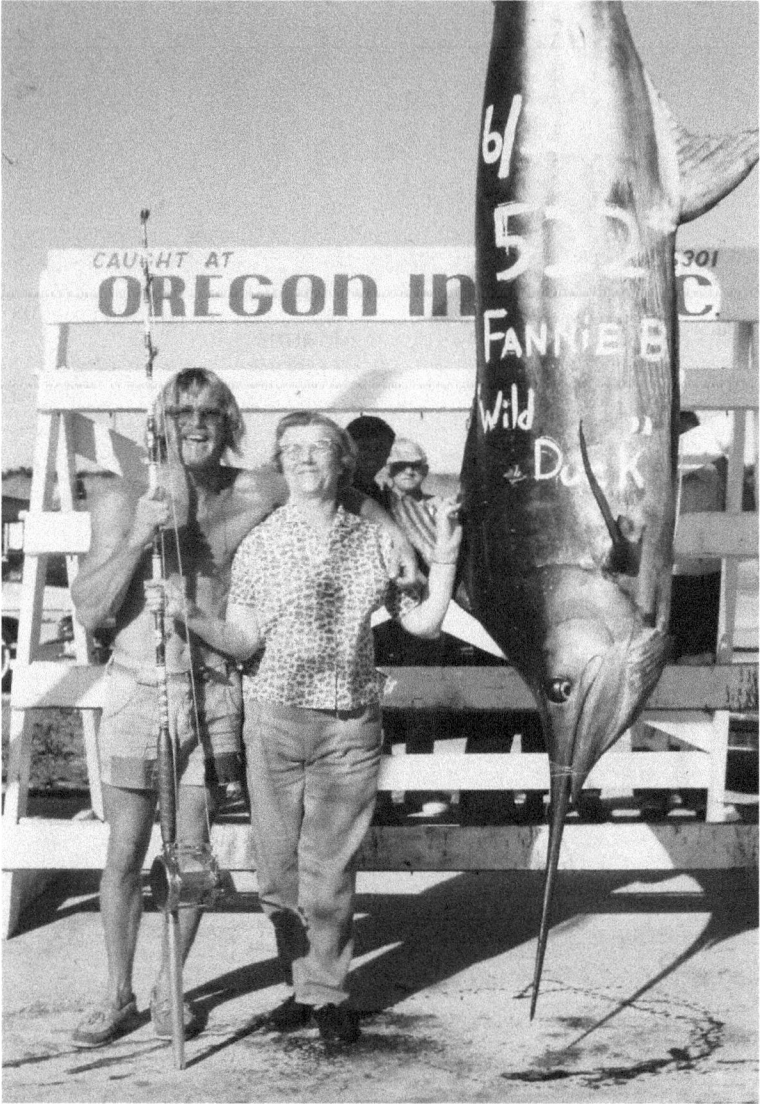

"My best marlin ever! My mother, Fannie Perry Baum, at age 65, caught this 522 pounder in 1975. Murray Cudworth and I took her out on the *Wild Duck*. We hooked him in twenty fathoms of water on the way in and put him in the boat in less than 30 minutes. My mother was winding the reel so fast I was afraid she was going to have a heart attack."
Charles Perry

Foreword

BY CHARLES PERRY

My career on the water had an early start. My mother first knew I could crawl when I got out of the wooden fish box being used as a crib and crawled into the cabin of my father's charter boat, the Maggie. Capt. Charlie Perry married late in life and was fifty-five when I was born. When I was six, I started mating for him on weekends. That was the end of my earning pins for church attendance!

I fished inshore until I was fourteen, then started fishing offshore. I fished every summer out of Oregon Inlet through high school and the first two years of college. During my little government paid vacation (1969-1970), R & R in Australia ignited a desire to travel and fish the hot spots around the world. I have slowed down after sixty years of fishing worldwide, but I haven't stopped. Few people have the opportunity to make a life doing something they truly love!

Throughout my early years of traveling, other fishermen invariably asked where I was from and what kind of fishing could be found in my home area. I would tell them about the proximity of the Outer Banks to the Gulf Stream and the great variety of migratory fish available. The Outer Banks has now become very well-known, and captains from other fishing locations frequently ask me if I can find them an "Outer Banks mate." They know that a mate from Oregon Inlet or Hatteras will have experience catching a variety of fish, will know how to work hard and show up on time each day, and will socialize well with the charters.

This is why my friend Capt. Fin Gaddy (of the charter boat the *Qualifier*) and I agreed on the need for a written history about how sportfishing first got started here on the Outer Banks and how it led to

7

the development of the finest boatbuilding industry in the world. Of all my travels in the sportfishing world, I have never seen another place that surpasses our year-round quality fishing and superb boatbuilding.

My research for this book included the distinct pleasure of interviewing captains and mates who started the transition to recreational fishing on the Outer Banks. Their shared memories capture this history and how it led to the building of better boats, safer and more comfortable for the charters.

These pioneering charter captains would fish during the summer and build boats during the winter. Capt. Warren O'Neal, one of the early boat builders, hired other captains to help him during the winter months. As the workers gained more experience, they started building boats on their own. When fishing their recently built boats during the summer, these captains would look for ways to tweak their next boat to make it better. Over the years, these boats have developed a reputation of being some of the finest sportfishing boats in the world. These vessels are not only fishing machines, but they are also truly works of art.

This book is a tribute to the watermen who came before me, those who mentored me and fished with me, and the younger generations who continue to search for bigger fish on better boats.

Teenage Charles Perry putting dolphin in box, Oregon Inlet 1963

Introduction

Charles Perry's reputation precedes him when he travels up and down the Outer Banks, the 200-mile strip of barrier islands he has called home for his entire life. Through a career fishing for world-record billfish, Perry earned his designation as the best heavy-tackle wireman in the world. He can't even count the number of black marlin over 1,000 pounds he has wired, weighed or released over the years in spots ranging from the Canary Islands to west Africa to Australia's Great Barrier Reef.

Perry's status as a "living legend," a moniker given to him by *Marlin* magazine in 2021, is directly related to the vast number of fishing spots where he has brought in huge billfish over his seventy-year career. If there is a corner of the globe where big fish are said to be biting, it's a guarantee that Perry has fished there. Given that range of international experience, it's no wonder that friends and journalists alike are quick to ask him the same question: "What's the best place you've ever fished?"

His answer to that common query is as sincere as it is automatic. The most varied, challenging, and interesting place to fish for sport, he always maintains, is right in his own backyard. From the sheer breadth of the fisheries to the length of the season to the proximity of the Gulf Stream, Perry is confident that an angler can travel the world and fail to find a better fishing environment than Oregon Inlet and Hatteras Inlet along the Outer Banks.

As much as he has loved his explorations of distant continents and the friendships he has made in a range of ports, Perry knows now, as he surveys his still-active fishing career in his late-seventies, that he was in the richest fishing spot in the world when he was getting his start at the age of six. His father Charlie Perry was one of Oregon Inlet's earliest charter boat captains, and when little Charles turned six his Sunday mornings changed considerably; instead of going to church with his mother every Sunday, he was permitted to rise before dawn to go fishing with his dad. Those early trips ignited his love for days on the open water punctuated with the pursuit and capture of huge fish, and that passion never waned through a dizzying array of fishing adventures and at least three trips into the deep guided by a huge fish to which he had attached himself. (He calls himself the president of the Underwater Wireman's Club.)

Through it all, Perry maintains, nothing compares to Oregon Inlet and Hatteras, the two inlets that break up the string of islands located up to thirty miles from the North Carolina mainland. Cape Verde, Madeira, and the Great Barrier Reef are all spectacular at the right time of year, he says, but an angler has to hit them in the optimal window to have success. Off the Outer Banks, a crew can bring in a rotating assortment of the most sought-after saltwater fish on the planet—blue marlin, white marlin, sailfish, cobia, red drum, yellowfin tuna, and bluefin tuna offshore, with even more varieties for those who choose to stay in the inlet.

One of the things Perry loves most when he's traveling the world are his encounters with people who know the fishing world inside and out and have a proper appreciation for the diverse and dynamic nature of the Outer Banks coast. One day he got a phone call from a captain he knew in Cape Verde, the west African island nation known for its blue marlin proliferation. The captain got right to the point: "CP, can you get me an Oregon Inlet or a Hatteras mate?" From halfway around the world, this skipper was looking for a dependable, experienced second-in-command on his boat and knew he couldn't do any better than the mates trained on the Outer Banks.

That call from Cape Verde stands out to Perry, but it wasn't the only time he was asked to refer a mate or other crew member from Hatteras or Oregon Inlet. The word is out about these mates, because the Outer Banks coast offers such a uniquely broad range of fishing experiences, as well as an extended season that makes dependability a requirement. When the bite is this good every day, a mate better be accustomed to arriving at the docks early and staying late to make sure the boat is ready to go before the next sun rises.

Even though he isn't native to the area, Capt. Chip Shafer considers the Outer Banks ground zero for his fishing origin story as well. His family used to visit Currituck County on vacation from his hometown of Statesville, North Carolina, and when Shafer was a teenager his dad bought him a skiff for $125 and sent him to the coast to explore and fish in the little boat. In those days, before the tourist boom that shaped the area, the town of Corolla had seven full-time residents and Shafer used to amuse himself by watching U.S. Navy gunners shoot the targets they had set up on the beach there. He played around at fishing during those days, but he never could have imagined how the experience he gained on the Outer Banks would eventually catapult him to the top echelon of sportfishing.

When a bullet wound on the front lines in Vietnam landed Shafer in a rehab hospital at Camp Lejeune in Jacksonville, North Carolina, he befriended a captain named Paul Haddock and soon started fishing offshore with him. His passion for taking a boat out into the deep blue in pursuit of big fish was ignited and burns hot to this day, as he has been a captain himself for more than fifty years and has caught close to 7,000 billfish. Shafer has fished all over the world and his home base has been in Florida for several decades, but he attributes his adaptability to all kinds of conditions and his dogged work ethic to his early days mating for Capt. Emory Dillon off of Hatteras and, when he bought his own boat a few years later, out of Oregon Inlet.

"At Oregon Inlet we learned a lot," Shafer said. "There were some great minds there. Some of those guys were huge thinkers. But I think one of the things that we might have had that some of the areas may have had less of was a work ethic in fishing, a desire to really do the best job we possibly could. If you had a degree from Oregon Inlet you were kind of at the head of the class."

Well-trained mates—and those who start as mates and become celebrated globe-hopping anglers—aren't the only celebrated export from the fishing centers of the Outer Banks. From the time just after World War II, when a huge marlin catch and an industrious county public relations man opened the floodgates on the burgeoning charter fishing industry, charter captains initiated another new offseason pursuit—boatbuilding. The boatbuilding trade, born out of necessity, has become a study in regional innovation and excellence, as those who know the Outer Banks best have added and modified features of their craft to make them better suited to catch fish off that unique coast. Today the sportfishing boats created on the Outer Banks are known worldwide for their speed, modern craftsmanship, and suitability for intense battles with some of the largest fish in the sea.

Charles Perry, Chip Shafer, and their friends—the seasoned captains who have notched countless exciting days out in the Gulf Stream and labored for long hours shaping hulls from juniper wood and coating them with epoxy in stuffy boat shops—are part of a unique Outer Banks generation. In their lifetime, they have seen their beloved beach communities grow from isolated commercial fishing villages to vibrant tourist destinations, places where crews take charter parties out and give them once-in-a-lifetime fishing outings, and then create the same unforgettable experience for another group the very next day.

These are men in their seventies and eighties whose fathers ran the very first offshore charters, early boatbuilders who tried new things and now serve as the forebears to some of the most spectacular boats in the world. Their tales, infused with determination and creativity, make up a timeline that stretches out with as much character, color, and distinctiveness as the Outer Banks itself.

Toby Tillett (Tony and Omie Tillett's uncle) ran the early ferry from Oregon Inlet to Hatteras Island, early 1930s.

CHAPTER 1

Hatteras Beginnings

In the 1920s when Ernal Foster was a teenager living on Hatteras Island, the only way to make a living on the Outer Banks was commercial fishing, and the primary form of recreation on the barrier islands was duck hunting, which was a seasonal pursuit of a handful of wealthy men who belonged to the select hunting clubs located there. The Outer Banks was so remote that it was hardly considered as a vacation destination—limited ferry service, no paved roads, and very few hotels. So when eighteen-year-old Ernal was looking for opportunity, he moved to Long Island and got a job in the Coast Guard lifesaving service.

Back in those days, when a young Outer Banks native walked in the door of a lifesaving station anywhere from Montauk, N.Y. to Wilmington, he was virtually assured to get the job on the spot.

The Coast Guardsmen in charge of those stations knew that men like Ernal had better seamanship skills than anyone else who might apply, because a childhood on the Outer Banks meant the ability to read and navigate all types of water.

Ernal enjoyed his work up on Long Island, but after two years he decided to chase a more lucrative career as an apprentice plumber in the Hamptons. It was a promising pursuit for two years, until the Great Depression hit and he lost his job in the early 1930s. At that point he had a choice: Live in a tiny substandard apartment in New York City and stand in breadlines for food, or move back to the Outer Banks, sleep in his own bed, and eat fresh fish every day. Faced with that non-dilemma, he came back home to Hatteras in 1933.

Maybe because he had spent time up north and then saw his home county with new eyes when he returned, Ernal soon hatched an idea that most of the merchant fishermen on the Outer Banks viewed as pure foolhardiness. He had ridden along when his own father Charles, a commercial menhaden boat captain, took occasional paying clients fishing in the inlets around the Core Banks when the family had lived in Beaufort. And when Ernal was fifteen he had started a summer business with a friend taking vacationers from the mainland over to Atlantic Beach for fifty cents a person, since there was no bridge access at that time. He also knew of some early entrepreneurs, like Capt. Horace Dough, who had targeted the island's waterfowl hunters by advertising fishing trips out of Manteo for channel bass and bluefish.

Charles Foster, Horace Dough, and others had just scratched the surface of what could be possible if seasoned captains looked for opportunities to make money by introducing visitors to the abundance of catches that could be had in the waters off the Outer Banks. Up until the 1930s no one took fishing trips offshore, satisfied with the hauls of fish like drum, bluefish, mackerel, and stripers that they could find in the inlet. They used their commercial boats for the occasional charter trip with few or no modifications, and it was more of a part-time lark than anything that should be taken seriously.

"The handful of tourists who visited would occasionally persuade one of the commercial fishermen, such as Vernon Willis, to take them 'sportfishing' in his boat, the *Willis*," wrote Ernal Foster's son Ernie in a 2012 *Island Free-Press* article. "The anglers supplied the tackle and sat on wooden fish boxes. Outriggers were unknown and rod holders were non-existent and the 'catching of fish for fun' was viewed with great skepticism by the local populous."

Around the time Ernal Foster was trying his luck in New York and then making his way back South, Belove Tillett of Manns Harbor was adapting traditional round-stern shad boats into early charter boats, including features like cabins and removable chairs that weren't characteristic of earlier commercial boats but were appreciated by the early paid parties.

In Hatteras, it was Ernal who changed the way people thought of sportfishing when he came back from New York and started to consider the idea of designing a boat whose primary purpose would be taking customers on successful charter outings. Like every pioneer before and after him, Ernal encountered plenty of naysayers; people didn't think he could possibly make a living that way, especially when the only way visitors could reach Hatteras back then was by a lengthy ferry ride across Oregon Inlet followed by a forty-eight-mile drive to Hatteras Village on sand roads. Another option was driving to Engelhard, where they would have to be picked up and transported to the island by boat. There was also only one hotel on Hatteras at that time—the Atlantic View Hotel.

But where others saw obstacles Ernal Foster saw potential, so in 1936 he bought a large quantity of Atlantic white cedar (known in the area as juniper) and started approaching coastal boatbuilders with the plans for his innovative boat. According to his son, he was turned down by five builders because they didn't think his plans would result in a seaworthy vessel, with Ernal telling the reluctant boatbuilders, "It's my wood and my money, and if it doesn't turn out right, it's my problem." Finally, Milton Willis at Willis Boatworks in Marshallberg agreed to take on the challenge.

Willis Boatworks sat across Core Sound from Harker's Island in the area that was then the center of boatbuilding operations on the North Carolina coast. Harker's Island was the birthplace of the flared bow now known as the "Carolina flare," believed to be invented by Brady Lewis for his commercial fishing boats. Milton Willis, the founder of Willis Boatworks, was one of the most prolific boatbuilders in the state, constructing fifty crafts between 1945 and 1960. Ernal Foster commissioned Willis to turn his unique idea into a reality that he would name the *Albatross* after the giant bird, associated with good luck, described in Samuel Taylor Coleridge's poem, "The Rime of the Ancient Mariner." The 41-foot *Albatross*, which was completed in April 1937, had a price tag of $805 and launched one of the most legendary sportfishing fleets in Outer Banks history.

In the summer of 1937, the first official charter season for the *Albatross*, Ernal and his brother Bill hosted a grand total of four groups and charged them $25 for a full-day trip. Knowing that he couldn't make a living on charters alone in those early days, Ernal operated the *Albatross* for commercial fishing ventures in the winter and pursued charter clients in the warmer months. His novel business plan, like his boat blueprints, encountered a chorus of opposition questioning why this young man couldn't do things the way they had always been done. As he said in a documentary about the *Albatross* fleet late in his life, "They laughed at me. Said I was crazy to mess with it, that I ought to get back to commercial fishing. Real work, they said."

If the introduction of boats like the *Albatross* was one key component of an Outer Banks fishing revolution, another crucial development was the decision to run offshore in pursuit of the larger fish that many believed dwelled out there in the deep. Just off the coast of Cape Hatteras lies the series of underwater formations known as Diamond Shoals, a notorious hazard for sea vessels and eventually a key navigational landmark for offshore crews. Hundreds of shipwrecks have occurred on Diamond Shoals, prompting the placement of first a lightship in 1824, and later a lighthouse in 1966, to warn mariners of the shoals.

When Ernal and Bill were just starting to investigate the fishing possibilities off their home coast, they heard of reports from crew members aboard the Diamond Shoals Lightship who saw big fish that looked like they had broomsticks on their noses, Ernie Foster remembers. They had no idea what these giants were called, but Ernal was one local who was determined to find out.

In the early and mid-1930s several intrepid anglers, notably Colonel Hugh Wise of Princeton, New Jersey and Jack and Paul Townsend of Ocean City, Maryland, came to Hatteras in pursuit of the broomstick-nose fish (which were soon identified as blue marlin), but their efforts were fruitless. The first successful marlin catch off that coast is credited to a visitor named Hugo Rutherford, an avid sportsman from New Jersey who was an early member of the Manasquan River Marlin and Tuna Club at Manasquan Inlet, New Jersey. In August 1936 at Manasquan, Rutherford and his party on his boat the *Mako* hauled in sixteen bluefin tuna in one day, each weighing between a hundred and seven hundred pounds. In 1938, Rutherford decided to come south to try his hand at the waters around Hatteras Inlet, employing a local fisherman named Lloyd Styron to help him navigate and search out the bite on Rutherford's boat the *Mako*.

Rutherford landed two marlin on that trip, including one that weighed 590 pounds and electrified the tiny community of Hatteras Village. The experienced New Jersey fisherman befriended young Ernal, whose imagination was lit up with the possibilities of billfish expeditions due to Rutherford's success. But as hopeful as Ernal felt, he also realized that he didn't have the right tackle to make a proper run at such a huge fish, since a captain had to book more than four paying clients a season to invest money into top-of-the-line tackle and boat improvements. But as Tom Carlson writes in *Hatteras Blues*, Ernal and Bill made the most of what they had.

"The only thing occasionally holding back the Fosters, it seemed, was their primitive equipment. Most fishing parties before the war brought their own rods and reels, but Ernal and Bill had their own gear, just in case. It was homemade fare: bamboo rods with twine-wrapped grips and automobile hose clamps for reel seats. The line was braided linen. Twenty-four thread added up to seventy-two pound test, a workable strength for offshore fishing, but Lord help you if you didn't dry it properly; it would rot quicker than a fall tomato. What reels they had were clunkers with primitive star drags, if they had any drags at all other than your thumb."

Impressed by the setup that had allowed Rutherford to catch a pair of marlin, Ernal consulted the older man about his own spread and learned about the importance of outriggers. Outriggers were becoming commonplace in more highly trafficked sportfishing areas like Ocean City and the Bahamas, but when Rutherford gifted Foster a set of red-and-white striped cane outriggers for the *Albatross,* his was the first boat in Hatteras Inlet to be outfitted with them. The red-and-white pattern on the outriggers would become a trademark of all the *Albatross* boats.

With his new gear in place, Ernal began his own serious pursuit of billfish, a quest that paid off in 1940 when he hooked a sailfish on his way back to Hatteras after an unproductive day fishing in the Gulf Stream. "Perhaps that first fish convinced Ernal," wrote John Cleveland in his book *The Albatross Fleet*, "But thereafter he always maintained that there was good billfishing closer in than most others believed, and his remarkable record of success supports that theory well."

Even as countries across the Atlantic went to war, Ernal was impressing customers with his presence of mind, knowledge of the waterways, and extraordinary navigational ability with nothing more sophisticated than a compass and a watch. One of his most memorable stories from those pre–World War II days off Hatteras involved the day he caught his first of only two giant tarpon in his career captaining the *Albatross* fleet.

On that particular afternoon one of Ernal's regular clients, Mr. Creech, had brought a group of friends to fish for drum in the inlet, and the anglers were positioned on various perches all over the boat to get their lines in the best place for the frequent drum hook-ups. Ernal's arm was in a cast, and his brother Hallas was assisting him on the *Albatross*. One of the men, perched on the wheelhouse canopy, lost his equilibrium in the chop and fell overboard. No sooner had the man splashed into the sound than Mr. Creech hooked up a giant tarpon, which was leaping behind the boat. "Near pandemonium broke loose as he set the hook, for not only did a beautiful tarpon vault into the afternoon sky, but Hallas was busy trying to retrieve the frightened angler thrashing in the water near the boat," Cleveland wrote. "While Ernal maneuvered the boat to help Mr. Creech with the tarpon, Hallas [also Ernal's brother] was reaching out with a long-handled gaff to catch the clothing of the man in the water and keep him from drifting away."

Eventually the swimmer was secured and the party could focus its attention on the battle with the active tarpon, which weighed in at fifty-three pounds and added a dramatic verse to the long-running ballad of fish stories that are still told and retold around the docks and breakfast spots of the Outer Banks.

As he worked to build his charter business and kept an eye on the brewing unrest across the ocean, Ernal had started dating Hazel Midgett, who he married in 1942. One story from Ernal and Hazel's courtship days illustrates the extreme remoteness of Hatteras Island during that era. Ernal's friend Fred Austin was dating Hazel's cousin, and the two women lived in Waves, some thirty miles north of Hatteras Village. Not only were there no paved roads on that part of the island, there were actually no roads at all—just long, flat expanses of sand, sand, and more sand. One night Ernal and Fred went to see their girlfriends, sat on their respective porch swings for about an hour, and then Fred proceeded to drive back down the barrier islands with Ernal sitting in the passenger seat.

"My Daddy fell asleep, and suddenly he woke up and realized something was wrong," Ernie Foster said. "He said, 'Fred, you've turned around! When I dozed off the moon was on one side of us, and now it's on the other side.' Fred had dozed off too, had turned the car around and was heading back up the beach the way we had come. But everything looked identical at night, so he didn't realize what had happened."

As word spread about Foster's fish-finding skills down south, ambitious captains on the northern end of the Outer Banks sought to diversify their own commercial fishing operations to include more charter groups, according to the book *Carolina Flare* by Neal, John and Jim Conoley. Horace Dough had booked his first parties in the mid-1920s and then capitalized on early interest with newspaper ads featuring such headlines as "2,000 Pound Catch of Bass taken in One Day's Fishing." As he recounted in his newspaper ad, Dough's clients landed a literal ton of channel bass on that one day in April 1928. The 1930s were a decade of brisk growth for his operation.

Of course, friends of Dough's in the fishing community soon started planning and promoting their own sportfishing ventures, with captains like Clyde Hassel on board the *Clyde* taking charters out of Manteo in the thirties. But the true surge in the charter business out of Oregon Inlet would only really gather steam after World War II had ended and the U.S. had found its way back to the pursuit of peacetime diversions.

The attack on Pearl Harbor in December 1941 officially changed everything for men like Ernal Foster and Horace Dough who hoped to make a living chartering recreational fishing trips. The nation was wholly focused on the worldwide conflict, with young men going to fight and everyone else rationing everything they could in an effort to provide resources for the war effort. Rather than waiting to get drafted, Ernal signed up for the Coast Guard, serving in Baltimore, Morehead City, and Norfolk during the war years. When he went off to patrol the East Coast he had to say goodbye not only to his new wife Hazel, but also to the *Albatross,* which was requisitioned by the U.S. Navy. As the story was told to Ernie, the Navy sent Ernal official papers to sign and the captain just threw them in the wood stove. "He didn't trust all the fine print," Ernie said. "He just figured he'd get his boat back when the time came."

Ernal might have felt good about doing his patriotic duty when asked to loan his boat to Uncle Sam, but his sense of patriotism was tarnished when he was out on patrol on his Coast Guard cutter and he regularly passed by the U.S. Navy outpost in Beaufort, North Carolina. On multiple occasions he saw the *Albatross*, and it was always being used to host parties for officers and their girlfriends. Ernal was quiet and generally mild-mannered, but Ernie said the sight made his father so furious that once he had to be restrained by his fellow crew members from swinging around and ruining the party by ramming right into his own boat.

The good times might have been rolling on the *Albatross*, but the war put damper on the Outer Banks' budding sportfishing operations and obscured the spread of tales about 600-pound marlin triumphs. Hugo Rutherford's catch had been all but forgotten by people outside the confines of Hatteras Island, and captains from Hatteras to Manteo had more pressing concerns in wartime than helping wealthy people catch fish for fun. It was only when the war ended and people started to seek diversions to allow them to move past its losses that the vast potential awaiting fishermen and captains on the Outer Banks re-emerged—with new momentum fueled by improved infrastructure and an aggressive approach to publicity. Soon sportsmen all over the country would be drawn to the sleepy towns and endless beaches of Dare County.

Two Dare County legends: Journalist and photographer
Aycock Brown (right) and Capt. Ernal Foster (left), 1930s

Aycock Brown: The Messenger

A coastal location can have extraordinarily fertile fisheries
and innovative boatbuilders, but those assets will be nothing but
untapped potential if the rest of the fishing world doesn't know
the place exists. Today, a situation like that would warrant a flashy,
comprehensive social media campaign, complete with thematic
videos and colorful graphics. For more than half of the twentieth
century, all the Outer Banks needed was Aycock Brown.

What was supposed to be a temporary stop in Ocracoke in the
mid-1920s became a lifetime calling for Brown when he spotted
Esther Styron standing on the shore. Brown, who had taken
journalism classes at Columbia University and worked briefly as
a copy editor for the *Durham Sun* until his ineptitude for spelling
forced a career pivot, was on the Outer Banks to do a publicity job
for an Ocracoke hotel (and to transport some bootlegged liquor).
When he met Esther, he decided to stay.

As Brown told Dare County historian David Stick in a 1974 interview, he was accepted into his new community in part because he was one of the only Outer Banks residents who owned a typewriter. He prepared documents for anyone who retained his services, married Esther in 1929, and tried his hand at promoting Ocracoke to tourists, an effort that was dampened by the Great Depression. Desperate, Brown started a fishing column, "Covering the Waterfront," and distributed it all over the state. There was only one complication; he had never been out fishing in his life.

"The column just exploded," Aycock told Stick. "I made so many errors in it, and so many people wrote in, see. I got more or less a list of correspondents who were sending me news every week. …I never knew a damn thing about it."

From those inauspicious beginnings, Brown started to hang around Hatteras and Oregon Inlet, learning about the highly coveted species anglers were seeking when they ventured into the Atlantic each morning. When two blue marlin were caught off of Hatteras in the 1930s, he was there with one of his ubiquitous cameras. He often recruited a nearby pretty girl to pose with the fish. His burgeoning publicity efforts on behalf of his adopted home were interrupted by World War II, when he served in a civilian role at the Ocracoke Naval Base, but when peacetime returned he poured his considerable magnetism and energy into unearthing the hidden treasures he saw all around him.

By 1951, Brown was hired as the director of the new Dare County Tourist Bureau, and he soon earned the trust of everyone who made news on the island. If a crew reeled in a prize marlin or a bumper haul of dolphin, the captain's first phone call was likely not to his wife, but to Aycock Brown, who would drop everything to document the accomplishment, then develop and print the photo, write up a short article, and stuff the missives into hundreds of envelopes addressed to newspapers all over the nation.

Brown himself once estimated that in his first year on the job he sent some sixty articles a month out to seventy newspapers and television stations. By one count, his relentless efforts over the course of his career led to the publication of more than 100,000 stories and photographs featuring the Outer Banks in print or broadcast form.

The Aycock Brown Collection at the Outer Banks History center in Manteo contains a dizzying number of photos from Brown's years promoting the area, but also reams of letters he wrote to journalists, or to agencies that certified world-record catches that happened in Dare County. If anyone had an audience anywhere in the nation, Brown was liable to invite them to visit the Outer Banks. His dynamic personality meant that reporters took him up on the offer frequently, even if they would find themselves on the edge of the earth without much idea what they were looking for.

"Throngs of people have traveled North Carolina's Outer Banks because Charles Brantley Aycock Brown said to," *Virginian-Pilot* reporter Lorraine Eaton wrote in a 2016 profile of Brown. "Newspaper editors published slicks of bathing beauties draped over shipwrecks and driftwood because Aycock said to. And magazines such as *National Geographic* and *Life* featured glorious, multipage spreads extolling the barrier islands … because Aycock said to."

When the 1970s and 1980s brought a bona fide tourism explosion to the barrier islands, Brown was the catalyst. Once he got people to the Outer Banks, the responsibility fell to the captains to run fruitful charter trips and to the restaurants and hotels to provide good service, but he lit the fuse that made one adventure-seeking individual after another say, "I need to get out to the Outer Banks."

The sportfishing industry owes an incalculable debt to Brown, but he also gave coverage to everything from small-town festivals to beautiful coastal birds to live theatre. Three years before he took the job at the Tourist Bureau, an outdoor drama called "The Lost Colony" was losing money. Brown accepted a post as the production's publicity director, and audiences exploded. Thanks to Brown's marketing injection, a struggling show became the longest running symphonic outdoor drama in the nation. Whether it was a fishing tournament or a play, Brown drew media and visitors to the area with his unflagging affability and his innate understanding of how to customize his approach to his listener.

"Aycock was nice to almost everyone," Eaton wrote. "He gave holiday gifts to widows and bank tellers and kept a trunk full of trinkets for journalists, children, tourists, and politicians. The man who ran Manteo's Western Union office was a friend. When prominent visitors sent a telegram, the man notified Aycock that they were in town. Aycock would hunt them down in his Chevrolet with license plates that said, simply, AYCOCK. If the traveler was a journalist, he or she would be treated to a fat promotion package and perhaps front row seats to 'The Lost Colony.' If the visitor was a French journalist, Aycock might be wearing a beret."

Brown kept extolling the virtues of the Outer Banks far and wide until he retired from the Tourist Bureau in 1982. He died two years later at the age of seventy-nine, but his prodigious legacy is evident on every mile of coastline from Corolla to Ocracoke. In any spot where tourists stop and boost the economy, especially in the marinas where visiting anglers and their trusted local captains run offshore for another day hunting the big one or the tackle shops where they discuss strategies for the next day on the water, the unspoken subtext is a tip of the hat to Aycock Brown's ingenuity, steadfastness, and persistence.

Where it all began: Dykstra's Ditch between Nags Head and Roanoke Island, with the old draw bridge, 1940s

CHAPTER 2

From Dykstra's to the Inlet

In the waning months of World War II, Aycock Brown was stationed as a civilian intelligence officer at Ocracoke Naval Base, tasked with identifying the bodies that washed ashore near the Outer Banks island that had become his adopted home in the 1920s. Eventually, enemy submarines became non-existent in the area, so the patrol boat crews filled their free time fishing rather than defending the coastline. As Brown recalled in a talk to the Game Fish Conference in Nassau, Bahamas in 1959, one day a Capt. Coyle admired the windfall brought in by a military boat.

"I remember one particular day a patrol boat came in to Ocracoke literally loaded with dolphin, false albacore, and barracuda," Brown said. "That was the day that the water off Cape Hatteras, where the Labrador Current meets the Gulf Stream, was given a new name. Capt. Coyle said, 'It's no longer Torpedo Junction. Those waters off the Cape are now 'Gamefish Junction.' "

It's settled fact that no Outer Banks resident has ever had better public relations instincts than Aycock Brown, so he grabbed that officer's assessment and turned it into fodder for his fishing column, "Covering the Waterfront," which he had started writing for the *Coastland Times* in the 1930s and revived when the war ended and he saw the potential for bringing peacetime tourists to the barrier islands. Before long every angler with a big catch knew that they would see Aycock, usually wearing a Hawaiian shirt with multiple cameras dangling around his neck, at the docks ready to photograph the impressive haul of dolphin or tarpon or, even better, the blue marlin that had come up from the deep that day. And if possible, Brown would always recruit a pretty girl to pose in the picture as well, because when he sent his photographs to hundreds of newspapers all over the country he knew they might need that extra flair if they were going to make it from the mail pile into that paper's pages.

Brown's story of Navy seamen plying the waters off the Outer Banks for fish perfectly frames the postwar evolution of the region's gamefishing industry. Fueled by Brown's cameras and his typewriter, a well-kept secret of locals and a few intrepid out-of-towners started to mushroom in the late 1940s and early 1950s into a major sportfishing destination. Brown would report an impressive catch, newspapers would run his photo, and anglers would book their trips. Before too long the cycle was energizing plans for new paved roads, hotels, and eateries for local businesspeople who understood the potency of tourism on their islands.

On June 24, 1947, Brown wrote in his column, "In some of the Waterfront columns along about this time last year reference was made to agitation by the Department of Conservation and Development for expanding the sportsfishing business along our North Carolina coast. It was our contention that the idea was sound, and we shared the thoughts of several who believed that North Carolina coastal game fishing was a multimillion-dollar business if developed."

As Brown was transitioning from a military role back into his natural habitat of journalism and publicity, Ernal Foster was preparing to restart his nascent charter business, which he had started to build on the *Albatross I* before the war consumed the nation's attention. But before he could book new customers, Foster had to repossess his boat from the U.S. Navy. In 1945, he went to Portsmouth, Virginia and asked to meet with the commanding officer. When the two men sat down, Foster requested the return of his boat. But the transaction didn't initially go as smoothly as Foster had hoped.

"Sir, we own the boat," the officer replied to Ernal's request. "We've got the papers."

"I don't think so, because when those papers came to Hatteras, I threw 'em in the coal stove."

Ernal demanded that the officer show him the signed papers he claimed he had, and when the man couldn't produce the paperwork he unceremoniously threw the visitor out of his office. But such disrespect, especially when he knew exactly how his boat had been used by the officers during wartime, just warmed Ernal up for a fight. One of his Coast Guard friends had overheard the argument and was incredulous, warning Ernal that he might have just earned himself an assignment to a remote location. The friend told Ernal, "You're heading to the Pacific! That guy is going to get rid of you. You'd better find someone with some pull, and fast!"

As it turned out, Ernal did have friends in high places. Before the war, Congressman Herbert Bonner, a legendary advocate for the Outer Banks, had hired him on a charter trip, and they had hit it off. Ernal contacted Congressman Bonner, who came down to Hatteras to go fishing with a friend who just happened to be the commandant of the Coast Guard. Ernal explained the roadblock he had hit in trying to reclaim his property, and a few days later he was summoned back to the Navy office in Portsmouth. He knew everything was going to work out fine when he walked in the door and the commanding officer said, "Mr. Foster, would you like to take a seat?"

Just like that, the *Albatross* was back in Hatteras, where Ernal put a new coat of white paint over the military gray and resumed his charter business with renewed energy. The war had paused the momentum of his business, but with the burden of fighting lifted and Aycock Brown spreading the word, Hatteras suddenly seemed to be the prime destination for fishermen in the know. Starting in the summer of 1946, Ernal had more charters than he could handle, with bookings coming from up and down the East Coast. The parties that fished from the *Albatross* in the late 1940s included Pennsylvania Governor James Duff and journalist Bill Sharpe, the owner and publisher of *The State* magazine who also served as the publicity director for four North Carolina governors.

"On the threshold of the postwar Eisenhower prosperity, people with disposable income and eager for diversion started coming down once again to isolated Hatteras Island," wrote Tom Carlson in *Hatteras Blues*. "The same thing had happened after the Civil War. Northerners who had been billeted on the Outer Banks during the war had seen the seas and sounds crowded with gamefish. And so after the war, they came back."

It wasn't long at all before Ernal realized that one boat wasn't sufficient to handle the demand. Not only was interest in fishing from the *Albatross* brisk, the parties were growing ever larger, which facilitated the need for more than one boat for a trip. To accommodate this situation, Ernal would offer to pay local friends a portion of his charter fee if they let him borrow their boat, but if conditions were good for a commercial or a charter trip those friends were known to renege on the agreement on the day of the outing. Ernal knew he couldn't work that way; he couldn't risk alienating good customers and he wanted to direct his business his own way. So in 1948 he went back to Willis Boatworks with detailed plans for his second ship, the *Albatross II*.

Once he had an official fleet containing two craft, Ernal and his brother Bill were equipped to handle the demand for big and small groups alike, and their success led to new charter efforts popping up in the area, often as commercial fishing captains saw an opportunity for a new income stream from the burgeoning tourist trade. Ernal's son Ernie was born in 1945, just as the war was coming to an end, so his childhood was marked by his dad's thriving business—a rotating cast of charter clients coming from distant cities and the fish stories that filled the air at Oden's and other docks each afternoon when the trips returned. The other captains hosting sportfishing clients alongside the Fosters included Capt. Luther Burrus on the *Jackie Fay,* Capt. Nelson Stowe on the *Ursula,* Capt. Vernon Willis on the *Willis,* and Ronnie Stowe on the *Ronnie.*

Soon the Fosters were able to charge more than $25 a trip, as the demand drove rates up and they often found that they were fully booked and had to send clients up the docks to negotiate with other captains. The 1950s was a decade of pure growth and progress for the sportfishing industry in every part of the Outer Banks, but in Hatteras it is a legacy that will always be most closely associated with Ernal Foster and his *Albatross* boats, which became a trio when he commissioned the construction of the *Albatross III* in 1953. Right around the same time, the colorful Capt. Edgar Styron introduced *Twins* as the second charter-only boat in the area, and the next year he added the *Twins II* to the Hatteras fleet.

"Capt. Edgar was an outspoken man, given a bit to derring-do, and he was a great fisherman," according to a 2012 article Ernie Foster wrote about the history of Hatteras sportfishing for the *Island Free-Press.* "He caught marlin, lots of marlin, and he caught some of them very quickly, maneuvering the boat in what was then considered to be a bit of a reckless manner, but what is now accepted as standard maneuvering technique for fighting big fish. He popularized fishing on 'the rocks,' an area which is now known as the '230' rock."

The summer of 1951 brought the most seismic fishing accomplishment so far in Capt. Ernal's charter career. Ernal had been venturing further and further offshore, certain that another marlin would bite off that coast soon and that he should be the one to bring it in. On that June day, his younger brother Gaston was working as his mate, and Ernal was fixated on a marlin he had spotted the previous day.

He had been trying to upgrade his tackle in preparation for the big bite he was seeking, despite the fact that most of his clients still wanted to fish for dolphin and amberjack with the more traditional, smaller rod and reel. He had bought himself a 9/0 Penn Senator with 72-pound test line, and on June 25 he baited that rig with Spanish mackerel in hopes of seeing the marlin that he knew were out past Diamond Shoals. His customers weren't interested in blue marlin at all and let that be known, but that day Ernal was determined. He knew he could facilitate an excellent dolphin and amberjack haul for the paying clients and still have plenty of time to pursue a monster out near the Gulf Stream.

The fishing party was in the cabin preparing lunch that day when Ernal and Gaston, above the objections from their clients, decided to put out the mackerel, and almost immediately a blue marlin hit on it. Ernal ducked his head in the cabin and asked, "Anyone want to catch a big fish?" but they still didn't get any takers. As Ernal's friend Lloyd Styron said later he had heard the story from Ernal, "They didn't want to take the fish, after they saw him. It was just too much fish for them. They were older people."

It was certainly not too much fish for Ernal, so he called to Gaston to take the helm while he started his solo battle with the marlin. Ernal's stubborn streak came through when the clients asked him repeatedly to cut the line, but he was a true fisherman to the core and true fishermen neither give up on a fight nor cut perfectly good line. Without a belt or a harness, stationed on the *Albatross's* crude wooden fighting chair, Ernal entered into combat with the blue for two-and-a-half hours. The fish had died while deep in the water, so Ernal's triumph when he finally boated the giant fish was a reflection of his Herculean effort. The charter party might not have been interested or aware, but they were part of history that day—the third blue marlin caught off of Hatteras, the first caught by an *Albatross*, and the first to fire up the formidable promotional machine of Mr. Aycock Brown.

Just a few months earlier, a new entity called the Dare County Tourism Board had formed on the Outer Banks, and the local business leaders who created it had the good sense to hire Brown as the county's official publicity director. He had already been spreading the word about his adopted home for years through his fishing column, but with his new post he had the clout of the county behind him, with free rein to trumpet any significant event that happened up and down the barrier islands. So when Aycock heard about Ernal's marlin that day, he sent word that he would be there the next morning with his cameras. His photos of Ernal and his catch were soon copied, stuffed in envelopes, and directed to the mailroom of every newspaper Aycock could find an address for.

One party drawn in by Aycock's news item was a Richmond, Virginia couple named Ross and Betsy Walker. The Walkers were fishing devotees who read about Ernal's marlin in their newspaper and hoped the captain and his *Albatross* fleet might be the key to unlocking their own marlin dreams. The Walkers had already fished in Panama and other gamefishing hot spots, and Ross was born in Currituck County and eager to get back to the waters he had explored as a boy. When Ernal took them offshore on the *Albatross II* in the summer of 1952, the mood on the boat was strikingly different than it had been a year earlier. He was guiding clients who wanted nothing more than to boat a blue marlin. And it happened that day for the Walkers, but not without a little spool-and-line magic trick from Ernal.

Always interested in the trendy new fishing gear, Ross Walker had set his rod with a new type of nylon fishing line, which he believed would help their cause because of its unusual strength. But Ernal knew the flip side of the nylon—it was stretchy and might cause things to go awry during a fight with a big fish. Shortly after the *Albatross II* reached the Gulf Stream Betsy Walker hooked up to a good-sized marlin, but as she worked to reel it in the nylon line expanded so much that the spool started to jam the sides of the reel frame.

"Ernal had to do something," Carlson wrote in *Hatteras Blues*. "He grabbed one of his rods with twenty-four thread line, and took the risk of putting slack in the nylon line holding the marlin. In no time, Ernal had spliced the nylon line to his linen line and cut the line from the original pole so that the transfer of the fish was complete." But the drama wasn't over for the day; as the sun began to set and the fish continued to battle, the bamboo rod started to splinter. Eventually, with careful movements and a close eye on the faltering equipment, the Walkers and Ernal somehow got the 357-pound marlin out of the water and onto the deck. Betsy Walker was the first woman to ever reel in a blue marlin north of Florida.

Ernie Foster was just six years old the day his daddy and the Walkers caught that blue, and he and his mom were sitting in church at a revival service as the *Albatross II* motored its way back inland. In a way that's particular to small towns, word of the catch traveled fast, and Ernie said that someone whispered in the preacher's ear that he best cut his sermon short; the people in that sanctuary wanted to hustle down to the docks to see that marlin make its arrival.

Two big marlin in two years was captivating enough to pull the locals out of a church service and bring an ever-growing number of recreational anglers to the Southern Outer Banks, but Hatteras wasn't the only epicenter for the Outer Banks' emergence as a sportfishing mecca. Up at Oregon Inlet, a two-hour drive north from the *Albatross*'s headquarters, another group of ambitious captains was outfitting their boats and filling their own booking calendars.

At the same time that word of Hatteras's postwar fishing boom had reached Nags Head and the Roanoke Island communities of Wanchese and Manteo, newly available state funds were improving roads and bridges so that residents of Virginia and inland North Carolina communities could more easily access the Outer Banks. This combination of events led a group of commercial captains, along with some younger anglers looking to start a new operation, to try their own rods at the charter fishing game. Thanks to boatbuilders like Belove Tillett and Bob Scarborough, these men had the crafts to start taking bookings, but the missing piece of the puzzle in the mid-1940s was a location from which to embark.

Along Highway 64 between Nags Head and Manteo, there was a roadside canal with deep-water access all the way to Oregon Inlet and the Gulf Stream. The canal was named for George Dykstra, so when the local captains came together to create their base of operations they called it Dykstra's Ditch. The spot included a small store that sold fishing supplies and handled bookings, and parties could use the makeshift marina as a launching point for either inlet or offshore trips. Word spread, and before long the original charter captains were joined by others who had originally tied up in Wanchese or Manteo. By the late 1940s, more than a dozen boats were operating out of Dykstra's.

In those early days Dykstra's could only be reached by a dirt road, and Moon Tillett, who started fishing out of there in the early 1950s when he was twelve years old, remembers the crews using wood planks to get from the shore to their boats. It was a far cry from the sprawling, well-appointed marinas of today, but those early captains—men like Chick Craddock, Kenneth Ward, Joe Berry, Clarence Holmes, Les and Griz Evans, Charlie, Herbert and Lawrence Perry, Lee Dough, Dan and Rhondall Lewark, Fred Basnight, Will Etheridge Jr., Omie Tillett, Jesse Etheridge, and Balfour Baum—have inspired countless younger anglers as the trailblazers of the business.

Even legends have to start somewhere, and the man whose name is most closely associated with Outer Banks fishing and boatbuilding got his start as mate out of Dykstra's in the late 1940s. Omie Tillett worked with Jerry Turner on a Belove Tillett round stern boat called the *Jerry, Jr.*, which was one of the first boats to fish out in the Gulf Stream. Omie's father Sam Tillett had opened his restaurant back in 1937, originally calling it Sambo's. When Omie joined the operation a decade later it was renamed Sam and Omie's, and a favorite tip about the establishment was, "customers can order anything they want but what they're going to get is salty scrambled eggs, hard bacon, burnt toast and strong coffee." The current iteration of Sam and Omie's is still a favorite Nags Head gathering place, and it also serves as a gallery of the old photos from the earliest days of sportfishing in the area.

One of the other Dykstra's pioneers, Will Etheridge Jr., caught the first blue marlin from that part of the Outer Banks coast in 1953. Etheridge, who later operated one of the most successful family commercial operations in the area, was known for his incredible fishing prowess; from the time the Oregon Inlet fleet started keeping records, Etheridge's catch total was always at the top.

Among the original Dykstra's cast of characters, Joe Berry's name and legacy stands out, and not just because he was the only black captain in the area for years. When Charles Perry went down to Dykstra's and later Oregon Inlet with his father Charlie and his uncles Lawrence and Herbert, Joe was always one of the first to throw him in the air and let him help him on his boat. If a fellow captain had a mechanical issue or got caught in a storm while out on a trip, Berry was always one of the first to come to the rescue. And one story from those early days, retold in a *Coastland Times* article, sheds light on Berry's approach to dealing with fellow fisherman who made an issue about his race.

One day a group of the men were sitting together drinking after a long fishing day, and a captain who had had too much to drink threw out a racial slur about Berry. Some of the other captains reacted immediately, wanting to set the offender straight, but Berry calmly said, "Don't worry. I'll get him back." A couple of weeks later Berry was booked solid for the day and an interested party came up to his dock to inquire about a charter on his boat, the *Phyllis Mae*. Berry walked past five other captains to the man who had insulted him to give him the job. That day after the boats had returned, the man went down to the *Phyllis Mae* and said, with tears, "You got me. You hurt me real bad and you did it with kindness. Joe, you've got a friend for life!"

Moon Tillett wasn't one of the initial Dykstra's captains, but when his father died in 1951 he took over running his dad's boat the *Bumbalo,* even though he wasn't a teenager yet. Stories of boys who weren't nearly old enough to get a driver's license taking parties out for a day of fishing abound on the Outer Banks, and Moon ran charters for more than a decade before turning to commercial fishing. He didn't venture offshore in his early years, instead running trips primarily to catch drum and blues in the inlet, but he remembers motoring to the inlet and watching, amazed, as Omie continued out to points that were, at the time, unknown to Moon and many of his fellow inlet anglers.

Some of the original Dykstra's captains fished out of the canal for close to a decade, but it didn't take long for two members of the fleet, Charlie and Herbert Perry, to search for a location that was more convenient to the fishing grounds. In the late 1940s the brothers found a small creek on south Bodie Island, deeming it deep enough for their boats and more convenient to the inlet. As Neal, John, and Jim Conoley wrote in their book *Carolina Flare,* the Perrys were known for making the trip to this dock, which was remote at the time, as eventful as the fishing trip itself.

"They met their parties at 4 a.m. in a designated spot, drove their old station wagon down the paved road to Whalebone Junction, then traversed the last eight miles of their journey to a deep sand path where the party might have to get out and help push the car just to keep it going," Conoley wrote. The Perrys got to start sleeping a bit later in 1951, when the state paved the road from Whalebone Junction to Oregon Inlet, and in the subsequent years the designation of the area as the Cape Hatteras National Seashore and a series of improvements to the property led to the official establishment of the Oregon Inlet Fishing Center.

After the National Park Service took over management of the land in 1953, Toby Tillett was given the lease to manage concessions and ferry transportation for the inlet's fishing business, and from then on Tillett became an important part of the emerging sportfishing industry there. He had the creek dredged, added a bulkhead and a parking area, and built a small marina and bait shop. In 1956 he expanded the tackle shop and moved it to the north end of the creek, and the following year George and H.A. Creek took over the concession services for the center. Another key development during that time, the official organization of the local captains into the Oregon Inlet Guides Association in 1955, gave area captains a unified voice as the fishing center became a major business presence along the waterfront.

Even as eager anglers from all over the East Coast made their way to the increasingly accessible Outer Banks and found a growing cadre of qualified captains to take them out in search of fish, the boats that were being used at that point were still primarily modified commercial trawlers with maximum cruising speeds of ten knots or so. At that speed, captains wanting to venture offshore from Oregon Inlet would spend most of the day coming and going, which inhibited the sought after hunt for marlin. For the sportfishing industry on the Outer Banks to shift into a higher gear, the boats would have to catch up to the growing ambition to go further and deeper and hook larger beasts. A boatbuilding revolution was needed, and the very trailblazers who were leading the sportfishing surge were the ideal ones to make it happen.

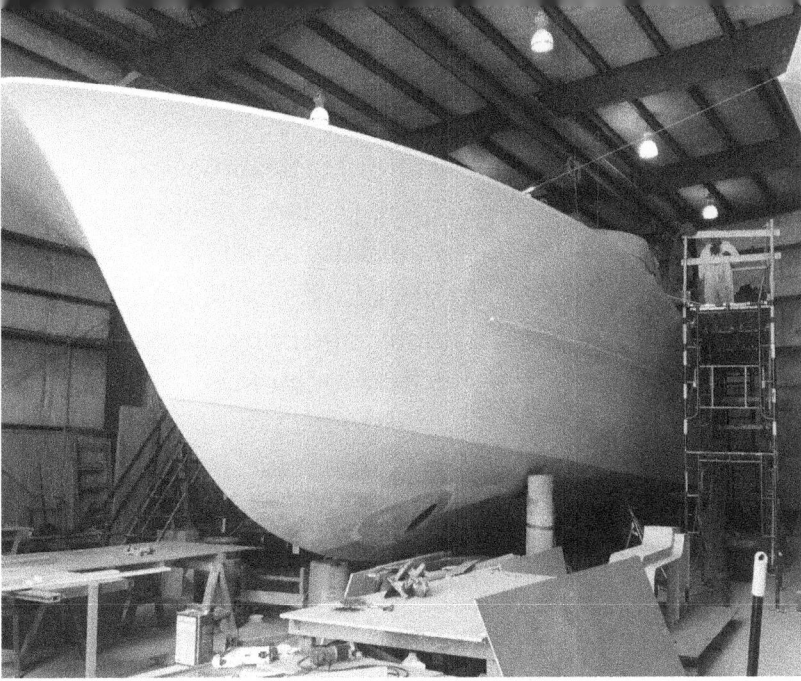

Hull under construction showcasing the "Carolina flare," an innovation that produced a drier ride

CHAPTER 3

Carolina Flare Origins

When Warren O'Neal was nine years old growing up in Manteo he carved a wooden canoe, complete with a dugout seat and a paddle. A few years later, when he was fifteen and hoping to make some money fishing in the inlet near his hometown, he built a simple flat-bottom skiff. He wouldn't officially be considered a boatbuilder for many years after those early crafts, but they were the first points on a career timeline that eventually launched a boatbuilding career that revolutionized sportfishing on O'Neal's native Outer Banks. His legacy, and one that has been built on in spectacular ways in the years since, was his ability to understand, through trial and error and his friends' advice, the qualities that would allow a craft to handle and attract fish optimally in those particular waters.

But despite the indelible nature of O'Neal's boatbuilding legacy on the Outer Banks, many people don't know about the life he lived before he started designing sportfishing vessels. When he founded O'Neal Boatworks in 1959 he was fifty years old, having spent most of the previous five decades fishing, observing, and gathering the insight and expertise he would need for his main event. "I always was amazed at the fact that he didn't really do what he loved until he turned fifty," said O'Neal's grandson Stuart Bell. "In a way, it was an inspiration to me."

Born in 1910, O'Neal went off to Duke University just before the Great Depression hit the nation, until the financial crisis forced him to withdraw from school. He moved to Chicago to work and attend trade school, and he learned drafting skills at both Duke and the Chicago school that he would later use to great advantage at O'Neal Boatworks. But for most of the intervening years between that patch-work education and his emergence as one of region's most influential boatbuilders, O'Neal was a commercial and charter fisherman.

He was successful enough on the commercial circuit, Bell recalled, that he was able to pay for the construction of a new house for him and his wife Pearl with the proceeds from one day's fishing—a huge haul of croakers in the mid-1940s. During that decade, he fished from a traditional round-stern shad boat, but in 1949 he worked with his friend Otis Dough, whose family was known for Outer Banks shad boats, to complete a juniper boat designed for commercial use. After working on it for so long with Otis, Warren decided to buy it himself and named it the *Pearl* after his wife.

Throughout the 1950s, O'Neal engaged more with sportfishing and settled into the seasonal routine many of his angler friends on the Outer Banks followed—longlining or shrimping in the offseason, carrying charter parties in the warmer months. A spike in his charter business called for some modifications to the *Pearl*, so in 1951 he upgraded the interior, added five feet of length, and squared the stern to better accommodate the growing demand for offshore trips. But even though he and his fellow captains at the

Oregon Inlet Fishing Center stayed booked during those years, the growth of the trade was leading him in a different direction. Too many captains were using commercial boats for charter trips, and he knew he could design a boat that would serve them better—one that was customized for speed, comfort, and effectiveness in the sportfishing sector.

So it was that O'Neal hung out a shingle for O'Neal Boatworks in 1959 and welcomed his first customer, Capt. Omie Tillett. Tillett and O'Neal were good friends, and Tillett had his own feelings about how a sportfishing boat should be fashioned. On a trip to Florida one winter around that time, Tillett had even visited Rybovich Boatworks in West Palm Beach to see some of John Rybovich's designs. Rybovich, who had built his first custom sportfishing boat in 1947, had pioneered new features like a signature broken sheer, a roomy and sleek cabin, an aluminum tuna tower, and a transom door; word had spread about the company's revolutionary approach. When Tillett came to O'Neal's new company and described what he had seen in Florida, the two men drove up to Norfolk, where one of Rybovich's new models was docked, so O'Neal could see it for himself.

Inspired by that visit, O'Neal and Tillett put their heads together and started drawing up the plans for the *Sportsman,* which was an apt name for O'Neal's first dedicated sportfishing boat. The vessel featured a broken sheer line and inset cabin like Rybovich's model, but with a flared bow, the "Carolina flare," that became O'Neal's signature. He had built flat-bottom boats in his very early years and had fished aboard plenty more, and as he said in a 1987 interview about his career, he had come to understand that the surf off the Outer Banks needed a rounder approach. "I started putting a deep V in the hulls of the bigger boats because it just seemed to me like they needed it," he said. "I had been running boats all my life and I knew what it took to make them efficient."

O'Neal's boats, starting with the *Sportsman,* were known for that deep-V hull that flattened toward the stern, which was necessary to smooth their running with larger engines and choppy seas. When the *Sportsman* was launched in 1961, it marked a sea change in the East Coast's approach to boatbuilding for sportfishing. O'Neal had successfully taken the best qualities of Rybovich's designs, made his own modifications based on a lifetime on the water, and created a boat that some referred to as the "O'Nealovich." No matter what they called it though, every captain soon wanted to experience the power and handling of O'Neal's inspiration for themselves.

Most students of Outer Banks boatbuilding history agree on a few features that distinguish a boat designed and built on their string of islands. For a vessel to be characterized as a "Carolina-style sportfishing boat" it should include all or most of the following: a flare on the hull, a broken sheer line, an S-frame, a deep-V forward, an exaggerated tumblehome (where the beam is wider than the uppermost deck), and a curved "hawk" where the bow, stem, flare, and foredeck come together. Bobby Scarborough, who started building charter boats on the Outer Banks just after World War II, modeled his designs after the early Chris-Craft boats from Michigan, which feature a distinctive sharp turn down on the shearline.

Even though every innovation springs from some degree of imitation, O'Neal was far more than just a northern manifestation of Rybovich. He combined decades of experience, inspiration, and a knack for taking a design from his brain to paper that, without hyperbole, changed the game for Outer Banks anglers. O'Neal was precise, drafting detailed sketches of his boats and even building small-scale models to check every measurement and line before construction began. As Neal Conoley wrote in his book *Carolina Flare,* O'Neal was the first local builder to "put his boat to paper." Conoley went on, "Most other boat builders used the 'rock-of-the-eye' method. In his customary humble manner, Warren explained that he had to see how a boat was going to look before he built her because he was not as smart or talented as other boatbuilders."

O'Neal was quite taken with the curved lines he started to incorporate into his hulls, so much so that his grandson remembers a time in the mid-1980s when O'Neal needed a garage built at his house but he was resistant to the idea of doing it himself. It was just a garage, and his granddad was known for sophisticated boats, so Bell knew they could get it done, but O'Neal just turned to him and said, "Son, once you learn to build in curves, you don't go back to squares." And with that, he contracted a friend to come over and build the garage.

Innovative designs and techniques were only one aspect of O'Neal's profound influence on the Outer Banks boatbuilding community. He also either directly taught or indirectly inspired nearly every major boatbuilder who came after him. Just like a successful long-term basketball coach has a coaching tree of former players and assistants who strike out and win on their own, O'Neal's boatbuilding tree includes such notable names as Omie Tillett, Buddy Cannady, Buddy Davis, Sunny Briggs, John Bayliss, and Billy Holton. Many of those men, like Tillett, Cannady and Davis, worked with O'Neal in his shop before opening their own operation, and others are just beneficiaries of his designs and techniques. It's no exaggeration to say that at least three-fourths of the boats going out on daily charters or competing in big billfish tournaments along the North Carolina coast were crafted by someone with a direct line to Warren O'Neal.

Cannady had already established a reputation as a crafter of excellent flat-bottom skiffs in the 1950s, but when he started working with O'Neal in 1960 he learned the advantages of adding literal flair, as well as other advantageous curves, to his boat models. The two men worked together on a new boat for Cannady's charter business, which was also O'Neal's second "Carolina flare" hull. Cannady named the craft *Mel-O-Dee* after his daughter and hired artist R.O. Givens to paint musical notes and staffs on the boat's transom. According to an article by the Dare County Boat Builders Foundation, word spread so quickly about *Mel-O-Dee's* artistic touches that more than fifty people gathered at O'Neal Boatworks to watch Givens work.

Like many of the hybrid charter captains/boatbuilders of the day, Cannady would build a boat in the offseason, fish in it for a season or two, and then sell it at a discount, working out the kinks along the way and making any modifications he deemed necessary to his next hull. Cannady specialized in creating what were, at that time, some of the largest fishing boats in the Oregon Inlet fleet. By the time he was named the featured builder at the Carolina Boat Builders Tournament in 2011, Cannady had constructed thirty hulls over fifty-two feet, all with juniper wood and the traditional plank-on-frame construction he had learned decades earlier from O'Neal.

The other renowned boatbuilder named "Buddy," Buddy Davis, was just a teenager when he convinced Warren O'Neal to take him on as an apprentice in 1967. "At first he was only allowed to clean the shop and pass materials to the carpenters, but he was quick to absorb the whys and hows of boatbuilding," Neal Conoley wrote. "Even during his time off, Buddy Davis would come to the shop and watch for hours as O'Neal neatly cut and fitted juniper boards." Eventually Davis was given the same job as O'Neal's grandson Stuart Bell: boat sander. "When I was very young, all I did was sand," Bell said. "My granddaddy would have a cow if I touched a tool. He said, 'You're a sander' " But the two young sanding specialists had different career trajectories after their time at the bottom of the O'Neal Boatworks ladder.

Bell eventually went to North Carolina State and launched a career in banking, despite his own teenage dream of becoming a charter boat captain. His dad, convinced he would never apply himself at the university with the sound of the sea in his ears, told him that he could use his college money to have his grandfather build him a boat, but when he went to see O'Neal with that idea, an emotional three-hour conversation ensued, with O'Neal emphasizing the importance of Bell forging his own path. O'Neal convinced him to try college and told him that if he graduated he would build Bell any boat he wanted to start his charter business. His career indeed took a different turn, but O'Neal made good on the deal nonetheless when he called Bell out to Manteo one day and presented him with a new fifteen-foot skiff.

Davis came to O'Neal not because of a family connection, but because he was convinced that he wanted to run his own boatbuilding operation. After three years of working on charter boats at the Oregon Inlet Fishing Center in the summer and as an O'Neal apprentice in the winter, Davis spent three years working and learning with Sheldon Midgett before opening his own shop in 1973.

Over the next thirty-eight years, Davis was one of the most prolific boatbuilders in Outer Banks history, with 400 boats to his credit before his death in 2011. He learned the fundamentals of Carolina design from O'Neal and Midgett, but he never stopped innovating on his own designs, materials, and techniques. In the 1970s he diverged from most of the old-school boatbuilders in the area when he experimented with fiberglass over wood planks, and in 1981 he was among the first to build hulls using a jig rather than the traditional plank-on-frame method. In 1987 Warren O'Neal actually paid tribute to his former sanding apprentice by saying, "Buddy Davis is doing things with boats that we only dreamed about."

The first Roanoke Island charter captain to collaborate with O'Neal on a boat, Omie Tillett, used that experience building the *Sportsman* to create his own boatbuilding venture, Sportsman Boatworks, in 1973. Unfortunately, a severe allergy to epoxy forced Tillett to cut that particular operation short. He might have only completed eight hulls, but he made his own aesthetic and functional contributions to the evolving form of the Carolina boat. Paul Mann, who has been building boats for his Paul Mann Custom Boats customers since 1988, told *Marlin* magazine in a 2018 article that Tillett's fingerprints are evident in his own construction. Randy Ramsey of Jarrett Bay Boatworks in Beaufort, North Carolina has also long credited Tillett as a key inspiration. "My designs and lines are still influenced by Omie — the traditional Carolina style with some softened radiuses and tweaks are still evident in all my boats," Mann said.

A few years after Warren O'Neal started revolutionizing his signature style, another Oregon Inlet charter captain started to learn the basics of boatbuilding during the winter months, and eventually he became another one of the local "godfathers" who would inspire some of the most successful boatbuilders in the next generation. Sheldon Midgett grew up making extra money commercial fishing off of his home port of Manns Harbor before serving a stint in the Merchant Marines. As he started assisting in boat shops he found that the carpentry tasks came easily, but he didn't start to think of himself as a boat designer until he happened upon an old boatbuilder named Stacy Guthrie on Harker's Island.

In a story told to Neal Conoley and recorded in *Carolina Flare,* Midgett recalled passing a home and seeing an old man working on a skiff in the backyard. Impressed by the lines and proportions of the boat, he decided to stop and meet the builder. They talked for a while, and soon the discussion turned to the process of boat design and construction. "The old man took a stick and drew some figures in the dirt to explain how he set up battens and frames to get the right proportions," Conoley wrote. "Capt. Midgett sat in amazement since this was the first time he really understood how to build a boat. He reportedly said that he learned more about boatbuilding in thirty minutes of drawing in the dirt than he had in twenty years of building boats."

That anecdote is a reminder of an era when tips and techniques were passed down organically, from one generation of boatbuilders to the next, and most boatbuilders were still part-time charter captains who completed one boat a year. There were exceptions to this trend, of course, notably men like Warren O'Neal and Buddy Davis who established extensive boatbuilding operations from humble beginnings. But boatbuilding was by and large a backyard pursuit, practiced by salt-of-the-earth fishermen whose innate understanding of what boats needed sprung from untold hours maneuvering all kinds of vessels in the inlet or on the Gulf Stream. Billy Baum, a successful captain for decades who custom built six boats for himself over the years and named them all *Dream Girl,* said it this way: "People wanted better boats, and as they fished they realized something that would make it better and then fixed it."

And new design breakthroughs weren't strictly the domain of the men who made dozens of boats a year in commercial facilities. Baum, who was known more for his fishing prowess than anything during his heyday on the water, created a bottom design shape he called "delta conic" that is used in Paul Spencer's boats to this day. Spencer always gives Baum credit for the innovation when someone asks him.

Sunny Briggs learned the craft from both Omie Tillett and Sheldon Midgett, with each of the boatbuilding giants guiding his own path in distinct ways. He was young when he worked in Omie's shop and he didn't have much actual construction responsibility, but that job planted a seed of admiration for the man that just grew through their decades of friendship. "Omie loved boatbuilding," Briggs said. "If the epoxy hadn't gotten to him he would have kept building boats. He was innovative in his boatbuilding, and also the nicest man you would ever meet anywhere."

When he was in his mid-20s Briggs moved over to Midgett's boat shop, where he had his first real building experience, although one of his early responsibilities was the unglamorous task of dressing lumber. "I've got a picture of me and Buddy Davis dressing lumber," Briggs said. "You didn't buy it pre-dressed. We had to run it through the planer. We're out in this field dressing lumber, and the pile of shavings is bigger than we are." From the time he spent in those shops and adjacent fields, Briggs was laying the groundwork to become a key figure in the next generation of boatbuilders.

When you trace the boatbuilding genealogy of men like Warren O'Neal and Sheldon Midgett, you understand why a tour of retired boatbuilders on the Outer Banks feels a bit like making the rounds at a family reunion. The list of Midgett's own boatbuilding "offspring" includes a member of his own family, his son-in-law Paul Spencer, who learned the basics from Midgett and went on to found the custom-boat company Spencer Yachts. But Midgett taught many others, including Buddy Davis, Billy Holton, and Tony Tillett.

Builders taught each other, borrowed concepts from each other and, when warm weather came back around, often fished alongside each other and competed for the largest hauls. Then big days on the water would lead to new ideas for better boats, which they would incorporate when the temperatures dropped and they moved back into their boat shops. This cycle of learning, adapting, and pushing one another fueled the charter industry, as better boats led to more productive and enjoyable trips and lured new tourists down to the Outer Banks every spring and summer. Warren O'Neal, with his vision of creating a new type of boat devoted to sportfishing, sparked a movement that changed the game at Oregon Inlet and far beyond. The legend of the Carolina boat started to spread to other fishing hot spots.

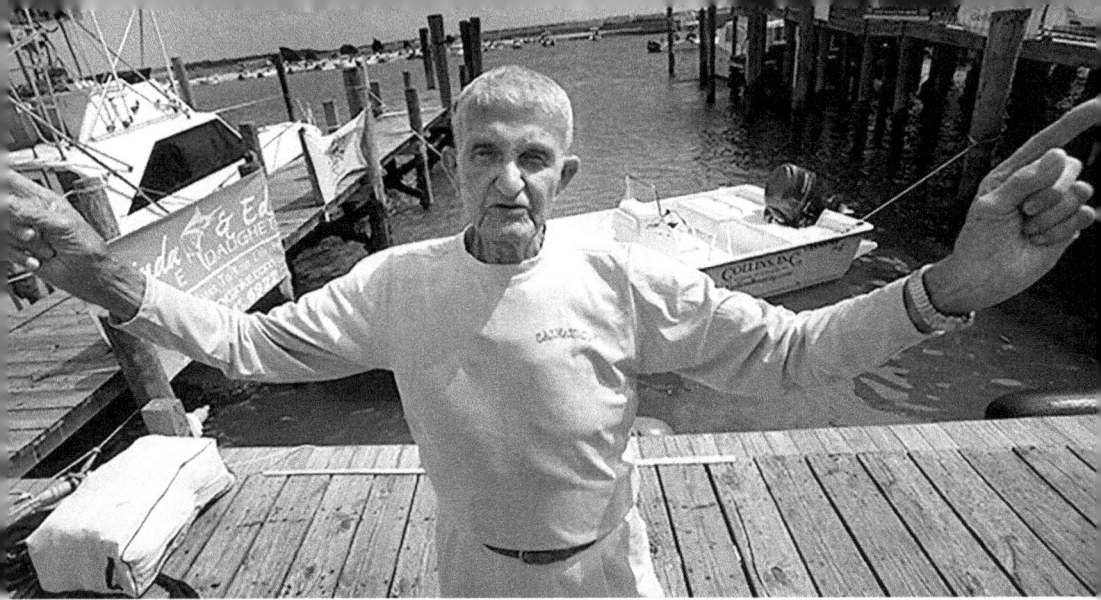
Omie Tillett praying for us all

Omie Tillett: The Spark

Omie Tillett inspired community among captains and boat-builders, but he also inspired friendly competition. He inspired hard work, modeling what it looked like to make the most out of every day on the water. He inspired perspective, especially when he prayed for the fleet before lines went in for a day of fishing. And he directly inspired one of the largest boatbuilding companies on the North Carolina coast.

It's no wonder that it's hard to imagine the evolution of Oregon Inlet as an epicenter of charter fishing and boatbuilding without the kind, steady influence of Tillett. Fellow members of his waterfront community from the second half of the twentieth century have myriad Omie stories, and the underlying theme of each is his ability to inspire those around him.

Born on the Outer Banks in 1929, Tillett stayed in school through the eighth grade until the allure of spending his days on the water became irresistible. His father Sam was a charter captain in the earliest days of fishing tourism, and he was also a small business owner who had started his restaurant, originally called

Sambo's, when Tillett was eleven. Tillett worked as his father's mate whenever he could, even filling in as captain when his dad asked him to despite the confusion of charter parties who thought he was too small to fill that role.

In his early teens, Tillett started fishing full-time, joining the earliest group of captains fishing out of Dykstra's and later from the Oregon Inlet Fishing Center. In the early 1960s he started working with Warren O'Neal on the first Carolina sportfishing boat designs, and in 1973 he opened his own boatbuilding shop, serving as mentor to a next generation of boatbuilders that included Sunny Briggs, Paul Spencer, and Randy Ramsey. He was known for his careful craftsmanship and natural mechanical knowhow, and even though his boatbuilding pursuit was cut short by an epoxy allergy, his eight hulls are still running offshore four decades after he completed the last one.

While he was undoubtedly one of Dare County's most prolific pioneers both on the water and in the boat shop, Tillett's enduring legacy is rooted in character, faith, and leadership. Like many other Oregon Inlet captains, Dickie Harris got his start as a mate for Tillett, asking for the position because he wanted to learn from the best. During those three years on board the *Sportsman*, Tillett forced Harris to learn by putting him in situations where he was in a bit over his head. By example and by giving him responsibility, Tillett taught Harris to trust himself in the cockpit.

Harris and many others in Tillett's large circle of friends admired his toughness, his adherence to his principles, and his work ethic. One time he fell on the deck of his boat, and when he caught himself he broke both wrists. Amazingly, two broken wrists didn't stop him from taking clients out in his boat every day. After Omie's death in 2019, his brother Tony Tillett, twelve years his junior, told *Outer Banks Coastal Life* about the advice from his big brother that had resonated with him the most powerfully throughout his own career as a charter captain: "Do the best you can, and make sure it's the damn best you can do."

"You didn't step out of line with Omie," said Sunny Briggs, who worked with Tillett as a mate and in his boat shop for five years. "You were never late; you always had a clean boat. The standard he set far surpassed what anyone else set, and he did it by example. He's the one who wiped the windows on his boat every afternoon, not his mate."

If a fishing day started out slow, Tillett never flagged in his efforts to generate a great experience for his clients. Paul Spencer, who also mated for Omie in his early days, believes that the hardworking reputation of Oregon Inlet's charter fleet today is a direct line to Tillett, who taught his mates that they could always try something else to catch fish, even if conditions seemed unfavorable.

"When I was fishing with Omie, when you weren't catching something you did not sit down," Spencer said. "You'd better be changing a bait, trying something new, putting out extras. Omie would tell me, 'We've got to crumb it out today.' And instead of pulling six or seven baits, we'd have to pull ten or eleven. He'd set up a whole spread here and another whole spread there and he would say, 'That little extra crumb will make the difference today.' "

Even if he refused to let his mates rest, no one has an unkind word to say about Tillett. As Briggs succinctly puts it, "I think Omie is the greatest man that's ever been." He always went to great lengths to help his friends in the fishing community, but stories abound of Tillett giving his time and generosity to strangers as well. Briggs remembers the day he heard John Mumford, a captain from Florida, come on the radio and ask about coming in to fuel up at Oregon Inlet. In response, Briggs heard Tillett's voice saying, "I'll be there soon." When Mumford pulled into the fishing center Tillett was there, saying, "You're going to need to get something to eat." Then he handed Mumford the keys to his truck and offered him some restaurant recommendations in the area.

"Omie had left him the key, and he had never even met him," Briggs said. "He didn't know John, but it didn't make any difference.

He was just another fisherman, someone he could help. He really loved helping other people.

He's the biggest influence I ever had in my life. I tell a lot of people, 'If you knew him, if you talked to him and spent some time with him, you were a better person when you walked away from the conversation.' "

As Omie grew older, his faith in God became the centerpiece of his life, and he lived out his devotion to the Lord in practical, undeniable ways. He was always quick to greet a friend with what he called a "holy ghost hug," and at some point he decided he wanted to start each fishing day by saying a prayer over the radio. This daily "blessing of the fleet" became an important tradition in Oregon Inlet and beyond; Tillett also prayed at the beginning of each day for the Big Rock Blue Marlin Tournament, and after his death Randy Ramsey, Big Rock board member and the voice of the tournament, took over the prayers in Tillett's memory.

Even though he lives and fishes on "the Crystal Coast" of North Carolina, Ramsey was every bit as impacted by Tillett as anyone on Tillett's home coast along the Outer Banks. After running charters as a captain out of Beaufort, North Carolina for a while, in the 1980s he resolved to build a boat of his own—something that combined the best elements of the boats he had encountered in his time on the water. The first person he turned to for advice was Tillett.

"He was always trying to change his boats and make them a little better," Ramsey said. "So when I got ready to build my first boat, I reached out to him to try to build a boat that was very similar to the one that he was running." With Tillett's feedback Ramsey built his first boat, the *Sensation,* and soon he had an order for another one. Today his Jarrett Bay Boatworks occupies a seventy-three-acre boatyard in Beaufort, and the company has custom built more than a hundred sportfishing hulls.

The ripples of Tillett's profound influence emanate far beyond the Tar Heel State to the many areas around the world where sportfishing has been enhanced by Carolina-style boats, hardworking Outer Banks anglers, or techniques learned out of Oregon Inlet. But the best tributes to his life are the less tangible ones, like faithful pre-fishing prayers and kind words and offers of help extended to fellow fishermen.

Hatteras Marlin Club in the early 1970s at tournament time

CHAPTER 4

The Billfish Capital

As Oregon Inlet was becoming a bustling hub of charter activity up north, a series of key developments down on Hatteras Island elevated its profile—and eventually its accessibility—as a fishing destination. Many of Aycock Brown's dispatches from this area in the late 1950s still focused on exploits of the busy *Albatross* fleet, such as a historic, and at the time puzzling, fishing outing captained by Bill Foster on the *Albatross* in 1958.

The clients were Jack and Elly Cleveland, a couple from Connecticut who had come down to fish on their honeymoon. They were also committed conservationists. On that day, the Clevelands and Bill shared the heart-racing experience of bringing in a 400-pound blue marlin. But when they got the creature to the boat, the Clevelands told Bill that they wanted to cut it loose.

As the marlin dove back into the deep, the newlyweds solidified their own role as trailblazers in the catch-and-release practice that would eventually come to dominate recreational billfishing.

The couple might have been confident about their wish to let the marlin swim another day, but as word of the release got out in the Hatteras community the locals, and even fishing enthusiasts far from the Outer Banks, had plenty of questions. In fact, news of the incident even reached the Big Apple; in a column in the *New York Mirror* published on August 28, 1958, outdoor columnist Jim Hurley wrote, "Here's one for the book—the conservation book, that is—an angler deliberately releasing a blue marlin! Boy, that's conservation practice for you: almost like a starving man refusing a sure-shot at a deer."

Of course, the Clevelands weren't starving, and their release did a great deal to further their cause. More than sixty years later Ernie Foster, who was just getting his start as a thirteen-year-old mate for his father and his uncle around the time of the Clevelands' catch, speaks with pride of his family's role in furthering the spirit of conservation on Hatteras. In addition to that initial marlin release, Foster also relishes the fact that the *Albatross* boats were responsible for tagging ten of the first forty marlin caught and released a few years later when scientists initiated tagging for the sake of research and conservation.

"It probably is not possible to convey the surprise, the shock, the absurdity of what Capt. Bill and Dr. Cleveland did on that August day," Ernie Foster wrote in a 2012 article in the *Island Free-Press*. "First they caught the biggest prize in the Atlantic, a blue marlin, and then they let it go — alive! Everyone was stunned to learn of what that crazy group on the *Albatross* had done. Captains smirked and writers wrote stories. The concept of releasing billfish had found its way to Hatteras as two men, one a highly skilled captain and the other a sportsman in the truest sense of the word, began a trend which is so entrenched in today's sportfishing culture that no one now gives such an action a second thought."

As word of charter trip feats, both those that returned with fish to show and those that did not, spread to distant points and other charter operations like the *Twins* boats owned by Edgar Styron and Freeman Stowe began to see brisk business as well, another new operation on Hatteras further cemented the island's reputation as a fishing hotspot. This development, which established an outpost for anglers that would soon become a respite for some of the state's most respected leaders, was first dreamed up at a Hatteras restaurant that was also owned by Styron.

The four men—Charles Johnson, Luther Hodges, Earl Phillips, and Willis Slane—met for lunch after a morning of duck hunting and sketched out a plan for a permanent marina and gathering place for the state's sportsmen and their families. The Hatteras Marlin Club would host tournaments, provide space for members' boats, and promote camaraderie, competition, and tourism on the island. These four avid fishermen weren't just Outer Banks weekend warriors; they were influential North Carolinians in their own right, and their prominence meant that they could secure the financial and community support to make the club a reality. The best-known Hatteras Marlin Club founder was Hodges, who at the time of the meeting was three years into his seven-year term as the sixty-fourth governor of North Carolina. Johnson ran a successful car dealership in Asheville, and Phillips and Slane had made their fortunes in the home furnishings and hosiery businesses, respectively.

The four founders soon turned their energy toward purchasing the property around the restaurant where they first hatched the plan, with Phillips actually buying the building and the existing docks from Styron for $57,000 and making it the centerpiece of the new enterprise. They contracted for the construction of boat slips and additional buildings to support their vision for the Hatteras Marlin Club: a gentlemen's getaway where fishing, hunting, and card playing would all be easily accessible. Bounce Anderson, who had previously worked as the secretary of the West Palm Beach Fishing Club in Florida, was hired as the club's first caretaker.

The Hatteras Marlin Club officially opened in 1959, and the following summer marked the first staging of its premier tournament, the International Blue Marlin Tournament. It wasn't the first fishing tournament held in the area—the Cape Hatteras Anglers Club started its own competition in 1958 for inlet fishing—but it was the first to focus on billfish and invite teams and individual anglers from outside the United States. To help ignite interest in his new club and its fledgling tournament, Anderson traveled to New York, where he encountered *New York Times* writer John Randolph. As Randolph recounted, "Bounce Anderson is hanging around New York giving to all hands the details about the explosion of big-game fishing in the last couple of years along the Outer Banks of North Carolina, while he whips everyone into a frenzy about the international blue marlin tournament slated for June."

Randolph went on to explain that the Hatteras tournament would start out as a release-only tournament, with 240 points given for any marlin caught on 39-thread line and 300 points for one caught on 24-thread line. "This is the right way to start any saltwater fishing program," he opined. After listing the other species of fish that had been found in recent years off the Hatteras Coast—white marlin, bluefin tuna, and sailfish, to name a few—Randolph ended his column with a comment from Anderson that captured the Outer Banks' scramble to create a tourist infrastructure around Hatteras that kept pace with the fishing discoveries there. "Anderson speaks warmly of the cobia, bluefish, weakfish, drum, and other gamefish in Pamlico Sound," the article read. "He speaks less warmly of the fact that there are not yet enough accommodations or charter boats at Hatteras."

The sixty-fourth anniversary of the International Blue Marlin Tournament, now called the Hatteras Marlin Club Invitational Blue Marlin Release Tournament, was held in June 2023, making it one of the longest running marlin tournaments anywhere on the East Coast. Hatteras Marlin Club has sponsored other tournaments over the years, such as the Hatteras Village Offshore Open and the Hatteras

Grand Slam, but before the club was even completed in 1959 another, more unusual fishing competition took place in Hatteras—the result of a war of words between the Outer Banks and the proud anglers of Puerto Rico. The fracas started in September 1958 when that same *New York Times* writer, John Randolph, became aware that both San Juan and Cape Hatteras had proclaimed their waters as the "Billfish Capital of the World." Randolph wrote a cheeky column about the competing claims, highlighting the surging popularity of the Southern Outer Banks as a fishing destination while acknowledging the historic prominence of San Juan's billfish bite.

A few weeks later, representatives from the "Comite Estatal de Pesca Deportiva" wrote a friendly letter to Aycock Brown, who had been quoted in Randolph's article as stating that seventy-eight blue marlin had been caught off the coast of the Outer Banks in 1958 up to that point. The letter countered, "Unfortunately, we do not keep records of our seasonal catch. All I can tell you is that—we caught twenty-two blues in the five days of our Fifth International Game Fish Tournament last month." The letter went on to assert that six hundred blue marlin had been caught in the San Juan area alone in the previous ten years.

Brown was, of course, compelled to reply. His bent for enthusiastic publicity never waned, so he filled his letter with commendations for the islands he called home and also issued an invitation. Perhaps, he proposed, the two areas could organize a tournament to determine which fishery really was pre-eminent? The Puerto Rican representatives agreed to participate, and the parameters of this unique event were sketched out and sanctioned by both parties. In a contest that the *New York Times* dubbed "The Great Blue Marlin Politeness Derby," seven anglers from each country would compete in two distinct four-day tournaments, one in June 1959 at Cape Hatteras and one in September of the same year in San Juan. When the Puerto Rican fisherman came to North Carolina their team caught more fish than the Hatteras team, taking seven marlin over the four days of competition.

The San Juan team also caught more blue marlin when the teams moved the event to Puerto Rico a few months later, but more total marlin were caught off of the Outer Banks than in San Juan, so it was a mixed outcome of sorts. The Puerto Rican team could claim a victory, but Hatteras Island got what it really wanted—a legitimate claim to a designation as "The Blue Marlin Capital of the World." It's a boast that still gets play in marketing materials and in Outer Banks gift shops today, but few of the people who buy those bumper stickers know that the phrase originated in a legitimate cross-cultural rivalry.

The Puerto Rico-Hatteras grudge match didn't become an annual event, but the tournament sponsored by the Hatteras Marlin Club grew and hosted anglers from Venezeula, Mexico, Bermuda, and San Juan, with the first winner, E.H. "Chilo" Bird, actually coming from the same Puerto Rican club that had thrown down the gauntlet to Brown two years earlier. Charles Johnson, one of the four founders of the Hatteras Marlin Club and its first commodore, presided over the event with pride. Johnson enjoyed a storied reputation along the East Coast's boating and fishing community; he once caught fourteen bluefin tuna in one day, and he had also won a boat race from Miami to New York.

As Johnson, Gov. Hodges, and their friends started to enjoy the amenities and opportunities of their new club, construction was underway on a marvel of construction that would join Hatteras Island to northern section of the Outer Banks and, by extension, the rest of the state. For decades, Hatteras Island could only be accessed by the ferry service out of Oregon Inlet, established by Toby Tillett in 1924 and then sold to the North Carolina Highway Department in 1950. The ferry, which Tillett had expanded from the capacity for just a couple of cars to a ferry that could hold fourteen at a time, made daily trips across the inlet, and for many years that was enough.

In another important development in the first half of the century, the superintendent of Yellowstone National Park had visited Hatteras Island in the 1930s and deemed it sufficiently unique in its features to warrant a designation as a National Seashore. Local leaders had differed as to whether garnering protective status from the government or leaning into commercial development was the right path for Hatteras until the Hatteras National Seashore was officially established in 1953. But those on either side of the question agreed that the construction of a bridge would warrant serious consideration before too long. Such a proposal became even more pressing in 1952 when a road was paved from Pea Island to Hatteras Village ending the long, disorienting drives through the sand that had bedeviled Fred Austin and Ernal Foster on their trips to visit their future wives.

The new paved road, which would become North Carolina Highway 12, originated in 1948 Hatteras Village with a 17.3-mile section east through Frisco and Buxton and north to Avon. Three years later, a 17.8-mile segment from Avon north to Rodanthe was completed, and by 1952 the remaining 12.4 miles north to Oregon Inlet were opened for motorists.

Suddenly regular travel down to Hatteras seemed like a more attractive possibility, and the number of people trying to board ferries to explore the island created unprecedented gridlock at the points of embarkation and disembarkation. According to a 2019 article by Joy Crist in the *Island Free-Press*, the Coquina Beach Day Use Area parking lot actually became a de facto camping area in the 1950s, where people would camp out overnight if they were turned away from the ferry, so that they would be sure to catch the boat the next morning. By 1955 the congestion had forced the highway department to run three ferries on the route, and that year the state requested funds for a fourth. Amid these negotiations, other lawmakers were hotly debating the proposed bridge across the expanse, which was expected to cost $2 million.

On May 1, 1961, Congressman Herbert Bonner, a Democrat from Beaufort County who served in Washington for twenty-five years, introduced a bill to the U.S. Congress asking for approval for the National Park Service's support in partnering with the state of North Carolina to construct a bridge across Oregon Inlet. After some debate—mostly related to the bridge's price tag and its future maintenance, which would come from the state despite it being located within a national park property—the bill was approved on October 11, 1962. Because Bonner had been a consistent champion of the project, President John F. Kennedy gave him the pen that he used to sign the legislation. Construction started soon thereafter, and the Bonner Bridge was opened the following year. At the time, engineers projected that the new bridge had a lifespan of thirty years, but it actually lasted much longer. It was decommissioned and started to be dismantled after the new bridge, named for another lawmaker, former State Senator Marc Basnight, was opened in 2019.

"With the opening of the Bonner Bridge, you could now drive all the way from the state capital, Raleigh, down the highway to the Outer Banks and on to Foster's Quay almost without taking your foot off the gas," wrote Tom Carlson in *Hatteras Blues*. "Access meant greater prosperity."

The bridge could not have opened for traffic at a better time, between the Hatteras Marlin Club's emergence as a social center and a wave of national attention from the friendly feud with Puerto Rico. Brown continued to type and snap photos furiously, and every true fish story brought more new visitors and prompted return trips from the charter customers who had become loyal to captains like those on the *Albatross* and newer entrants to the sportfishing business, men like Tommy Littleston on the *Lu-Mar*, Buster Hummer on the *Skipper*, and Tex Ballance on the *Escape*. "Early opponents of the bridge were correct that the Bonner Bridge changed the character of Hatteras Island, but they were also correct when they stated, 30 years before it was built, that a bridge would be inevitable," Crist wrote in the *Island Free-Press* article.

The summer before the bridge was approved, seventeen-year-old Ernie Foster was a mate with his Uncle William (also known as Capt. Bill Foster) when the two happened upon the catch of young Ernie's lifetime, further fueling interest in Hatteras Island's fishing offerings. It was June 1962, on the eve of the third annual Hatteras Marlin Club tournament. The two Fosters had been out all day with a party from Morristown, New Jersey that included an older angler, Ronald Sloat, who had made it his goal to catch a record-breaking marlin off that coast, and a young man named Gary Stukes.

Capt. Bill made a decision that was quite unusual for the time: to rig the line with an artificial lure. Captains almost always used real bait in those years, but a fisherman who had visited from Hawaii the previous year had given him the lure and asked him to try it out on a Hatteras marlin. He also had put a squid on his spread; as Ernie remembered decades later, "I had just rigged up the prettiest little squid anyone had ever rigged." As the party trolled they came upon a giant of a fish—looking to Ernie like a submarine as it broke the surface.

Sloat had been in the chair most of the day, but when he took a rest he passed the rod off to Stukes, who was in for the ride of his life. The blue marlin turned toward the squid but then changed her mind and hit on the lure, which Ernie had just repaired after the hook had bent on the boat's gunwale. Every angler who has caught a big marlin has experienced the instantaneous shift from a peaceful day out on the water to urgent chaos. Bill yelled that he had never seen a marlin that big before. Ernie steered the boat while Bill shouted orders at Stukes, who had never wrestled anything like the fish. Right away the marlin pulled off 100 yards of line, and, according to an article about the catch in the Norfolk *Virginian-Pilot*, jumped fifteen times in twenty minutes before it died near the boat and allowed Bill to grab hold of the leader.

"Bill, standing on the fantail of the *Albatross II*, grabbed the cable leader and sat down with his heels jammed against the toe rail," wrote John Cleveland in *The Albatross Fleet*. "For nearly a half hour the tall, sinewy captain held that cable before a flying gaff could be put in the fish, but the record fish was finally secured. The exhausted crew called for assistance from a nearby boat, and a strong, young friend hopped aboard to help."

Stukes, the inexperienced angler who was just giving his friend a breather, suddenly found himself in the record books, and the *Albatross* fleet had its own share of history. By the time the boat had finally docked at the Hatteras Marlin Club, throngs of people from the tournament's opening night dinner had poured out of the building to watch the weigh-in, and they weren't disappointed. The marlin weighed a whopping 810 pounds, setting a world record and giving Brown his marching orders for weeks. "The pictures of that fish went berserk," Ernie Foster said.

That 810-pounder knocked a 780-pound marlin from the top of the world leaderboard, and that previous record fish was caught by an angler in—where else?—Puerto Rico. As Jimmy Mays concluded in the *Virginian-Pilot*, "And thus was written another fantastic chapter in the history of Gamefish Junction. Let no man now dispute Hatteras's claim to the title, 'Blue Marlin Capital of the World.' The proof is now a matter of record."

A big day at in Oregon Inlet in August 1987. What a collection of great captains and large blue marlin!

CHAPTER 5

A Tournament Every Day

With a secure claim to bragging rights over Puerto Rico, an 810-pound marlin in the books, and a new bridge connecting the two prime fishing spots on the chain of islands, the Outer Banks was poised for a dramatic surge in visitors, accompanied by the type of development that supports and boosts tourism. Outside interest had been on the rise for several years even before the completion of the Bonner Bridge, with the North Carolina advertising division finding it necessary in 1955 to release an "information bulletin" called "The Rapidly Changing Outer Banks of North Carolina" as a supplement to its *Outer Banks Pamphlet*, which was less than two years old.

The supplement was warranted by the new transportation possibilities that had either started operating or were under construction, as well as the assertion that the "motor court and restaurant capacity" on Hatteras Island had more than doubled in the two years since the original pamphlet was published. Individual charter operations and marinas quickly came to realize that public relations had to be part of their business operation too, especially with so many newcomers who had not yet established a loyalty to a specific charter company, hotel, or breakfast spot. In one early advertising spot put out by the Oregon Inlet Fishing Center, the reader is dramatically transported out to the Gulf Stream where he's fighting a pitched battle with a series of hungry fish.

"The boat slows to an idle and the clear purple water turns yellow and fluorescent blue with dolphin," the promotional flyer said. "They're everywhere, and starving. They bite as fast as you can get a bait over and the fish box is soon filled. Now the big baits go over. This is what it's all about. You're after billfish…blue marlin, white marlin, or sails…And then suddenly, there he is, behind the long rigger. The fish crashes the bait and goes off grey-hounding in long leaping jumps. It's a blue one and he's tearing the ocean up."

If they found their way into the right hands, advertising pieces like that one would surely draw some ardent anglers with deep pockets. And it wasn't just the state's in-house publicity efforts that were touting the vacation potential of the Outer Banks; both *National Geographic* and *Sports Illustrated* published pieces in 1955 highlighting the newly accessible destination, with the *Sports Illustrated* story describing a drum fishing trip the author took off of Oregon Inlet.

The poetic opening paragraph of the article, written by Paul Gallico, almost certainly sparked hundreds of vacation plans on its own: "Picture a clear stretch of shimmering aquamarine-blue Atlantic, a hundred yards or so from a beach of dazzling whiteness off the North Carolinian coast, hard by Oregon Inlet, the gateway to Albemarle Sound. To the north stretch the grass-tufted sand dunes, rising to Kill Devil Hills at Kitty Hawk, whence the Wright brothers took off on man's first powered flight. To the south the sands curve to Hatteras." And travel writers didn't have to book a charter to describe the Outer Banks' manifold attractions; in 1959 the magazine published by the Automobile Club of Michigan got into the act as well, focusing on the new paved roads and Toby Tillett's efficient ferry service that had eased travel in an area that had seemed inaccessibly remote just a decade earlier.

As the Puerto Rico competition had demonstrated, marlin fishermen tend to hear fish stories from billfish hot spots no matter how distant, so although Aycock Brown only sent his pictures to U.S. papers, word was spreading internationally. In March 1965, Brown received a letter from a Dr. J.H. Kuhn, Chairman of the Transvaal Game Fishing Association in Germiston, South Africa. Dr. Kuhn recounted his nation's own established status as a billfish hotbed and inquired whether similar conditions might be found off the Outer Banks. In his response, Brown pointed the doctor to an extensive talk he had given a few years earlier at the Game Fish Conference at the Bahamas, in which he outlined the history, trends, and developments in the world of gamefishing along North Carolina's barrier islands.

"I believe, and there are others here whom I think will agree with me, that the fabulous fishing along our section of the Atlantic Coast at Hatteras is worth recording, and I will try to give you a word picture of how it all came about," Brown had told the group. "I do not have the exact score, but during the past ten years it is a safe bet that almost 500 blue marlin have been boated from waters within daylight trolling distance of Hatteras."

Soon the Outer Banks exerted a magnetic pull on individuals who sensed a range of burgeoning business opportunities. Sunny Briggs lived in Georgia and Texas in his early years, but when he was eleven years old his parents bought the Croatan Hotel, which at the time was one of the few hotels near Oregon Inlet. Briggs remembers his dad staying busy shuttling groups of hotel guests down to the fishing center in the mornings for their scheduled trips and then picking them up in the afternoons. He was spellbound by the stories he heard around the Croatan—tales of custom boats running offshore and coming back with marlin weighing hundreds of pounds. Briggs spent his summers on the Outer Banks, and even though he knew his daddy didn't have the extra money to hire a charter, he let it be known often that he wanted nothing more than to ride or work on one of those boats. When he was twelve years old his dad handed him three dollars and said, "You're smart enough to make your own money." So he asked the legendary Capt. Lee Perry, who ducked into the Croatan Hotel often to get band-aids for his fingers, if he needed a mate.

Briggs was one of a new generation, a group of up-and-coming sportfishermen who would hang out at the Hatteras or Oregon Inlet docks for hours like other boys might watch a baseball game, eager to see the day's haul for themselves. New charter operations were opening every week during the peak tourist season, and along with the brisk pace of hired sportfishing ventures, this period was also marked by a new emphasis on fishing as a sanctioned competitive pursuit. A new wave of fishing tournaments on the Outer Banks created platforms for crews to bring in a big fish in a high-profile setting—and win some prizes for a day out on the water.

A few inlet tournaments, like the Nags Head Inter-Club Surf Fishing Tournament that started in 1952, predated the tourism explosion sparked by introduction of new roads and the Bonner Bridge. At the southern end of the Outer Banks the Cape Hatteras Anglers Club surf fishing invitational, started in 1958, had grown over the past sixty years to a field of 600 competitors. But even as the quest for fish like croakers, bluefish, drum and flounder drew locals and visitors alike, a new breed of competition was gaining momentum with every new marlin conquest. In the 1960s and 1970s, tournaments started to coalesce around that most coveted offshore fishing trophy: the big billfish.

Spurred by the political and economic influence of men like Luther Hodges and Charles Johnson, the Hatteras Marlin Club's International Blue Marlin Tournament (which was renamed the

Blue Marlin Release Tournament in the 1970s) created a new standard for an event designed to draw anglers with their eye on a giant prize. Today tournaments like the Big Rock Blue Marlin Tournament in Morehead City, North Carolina and the White Marlin Open in Ocean City, Maryland feature hundreds of boats and offer multimillion dollar purses for one large fish, but in the early days the prize money was relatively modest. Tournament entries were motivated less by financial interests and more by the desire to have your proud picture, next to a fish nearly as tall as you were, mounted on the wall of the Hatteras Marlin Club or another respected coastal clubhouse. At first, the entry fee for the Hatteras Marlin Club tournament was $250, and the prizes were minimal.

The Hatteras Marlin Club tournament's social events were also almost certainly a backdrop for some weighty business and political negotiations. You couldn't sit down for a summer dinner at the club in the 1960s without spotting a distinguished person; members during that time included U.S. Senator B. Everett Jordan and his son, Congressman Herbert C. Bonner whose name would soon be forever linked with the area's famous bridge, North Carolina State Senator Lindsay Warren, and Conrad L. Wirth, director of the National Park Service. From its inception, the tournament drew a mix of private and charter boats, and entries came from areas up and down the East Coast. Charter captains like Ernal and Bill Foster were booked solid each June when the tournament rolled around, as would-be marlin champions learned which captains had the most offshore experience in those waters and eagerly reserved a spot on their boats in hopes of tournament glory.

As might be expected in a small village known as the Marlin Capital of the World, anglers have long coveted the trophy that goes to the Hatteras Marlin Club tournament champion. The event is well-known and highly respected, but the organizers have resisted the urge to expand it beyond the founders' original vision, a small invitational held for the benefit of members and their guests. The number of entrants is limited by the number of slips at Hatteras

Marlin Club and nearby Oden's Dock, Styron said. The smallest tournament had twenty-four boats in the fleet, and today it still only fields about forty teams.

While just a few dozen boats competed in the beginning, the tournament's reputation grew at such a pace that journalist Fran Gariglio, who visited the event in 1976 and wrote about it for the *Rocky Mount Telegram*, called it "the fisherman's sporting contest equivalent in prestige to the golfer's Augusta Masters." In his article, Giglio painted a vivid portrait of Hatteras Marlin Club manager Edison Meekins, who oversaw the club from its creation in 1959 to 1980. "Edison Meekins, club manager for seventeen years, has the physical appearance of a sea captain, who with his square-trimmed salt and pepper shaded beard and stocky physique, appears to have just stepped out of one of Hemingway's novels of the sea," the article read.

The first two champions of the International Blue Marlin Tournament hailed from Puerto Rico and Miami. As time went on, however, the winners' hometowns moved progressively closer to the site of the event. More often than not, the winners have come either from the North Carolina coast or from nearby states; as the number of offshore fishing opportunities in the area multiplied so did the proficiency of local anglers in locating and boating the prized billfish.

But while the tournament's hall of fame has become less diverse geographically over the years, Giglio pointed out that even in the 1970s women anglers were making a splash in competitive marlin fishing. "Before any women libbers protest the male conglomerate in big-game fishing, Mary Merritt of the *Germel* can boast of her conquest," he wrote of a big catch at the 1976 event. "Mary's 395-pound blue marlin rewarded her with the largest fish boated by a woman." Even well into the twenty-first century, women are a rarity in the fleet for big billfish tournaments, but in the past several decades women's tournaments, like the Alice Kelly Memorial at Pirate's Cove and the Keli Wagner Lady Angler in Morehead City, have presented unique opportunities for women to gain competitive offshore experience.

The Hatteras Marlin Club tournament became a release-only event in 1975, precipitating its name change to the Blue Marlin Release Tournament. As former club manager Homer Styron recalls, the movement away from killing billfish was gradual, and eventually the impetus for changing the tournament's rules came from Mickey Hayes, who pushed for a release policy when he became the tournament director. Before that, Styron said, "There were so many of them caught, and we killed every one of them. I remember when the *Happy Hooker* caught one over 600 pounds, killed it, and dragged it to the weigh station. Mickey was throwing a fit. I told him, 'You're not tournament chairman yet.'"

With the sixty-third staging of the event in June 2023, the Hatteras Marlin Club can boast its status as the longest-running marlin tournament on the Outer Banks by a wide margin, but the second-oldest tournament originated from a Manteo marina that sprung up almost by accident in the early 1980s. One firsthand perspective on the origin of the Pirate's Cove Marina came from JB Feinman, an Outer Banks charter captain who fished out of the center before it had either a name or a building.

As Feinman wrote in a Facebook tribute to his friend Brad Gillam, who bought the 46-footer *Carolinian* around 1980 and made Feinman the boat's captain, Gillam had the fishing boat he wanted but was struggling to secure a slip at Oregon Inlet. So he improvised, telling Feinman that he had a slip on the causeway in Manteo. Feinman didn't know what he was talking about, so Gillam took him to see the place. "There was a headboat Alan Foreman just put in there. And that was it," Feinman wrote. "Brad pointed to the only other slip there, three pilings on either side. No dock. No finger pier. Just a sandy dusty parking lot right off the causeway."

The two men came up with an ingenious marketing plan: First build a fish rack right along the causeway, then go out and catch plenty of fish and hang them on the rack where passersby couldn't miss them. When people stopped to see the fish, the *Carolinian* crew offered to take them out on a charter, emphasizing that they could go fishing right there rather than drive twelve more miles to Oregon Inlet. It worked; they ran successful charters for two seasons "out of those six pilings," as Feinman said, and that initial burst of activity sparked the eventual construction of the Pirate's Cove Marina. Before Pirate's Cove was even completed, in 1984 the anglers there created a tournament of their own, the Pirate's Cove Billfish Tournament. Pirate's Cove has added a number of specialty tournaments as well over time, from the Alice Kelly women's event to contests for junior anglers. In 2008, eight separate fishing competitions were held out of the marina in one season.

Between the founding of the Hatteras Marlin Club and Pirate's Cove tournaments, Oregon Inlet sponsored a billfish tournament, but it only lasted for about three years. The first annual Oregon Inlet Billfish Tournament was held in late September in 1976, but the competition was short-lived. Eventually the charter business in the area was booked so solid that it was no longer possible to block out dates for a tournament. Visitors who follow tournament fishing closely often find it surprising that Oregon Inlet isn't the site of an annual event, said Outer Banks native and legendary wireman Charles Perry, but he always tells them that the captains who run out of the fishing center there have created a unique take on a tournament—one that pits one half of the marina against the other and lasts for the entire fishing season.

Since the days of Dykstra's Ditch, the captains who call Oregon Inlet home have held to a high standard of excellence and, like most fishermen, measured their own daily catches against those of their dockmates. This spirit of mostly friendly competition, according to Perry, came directly from Omie and Tony Tillett, who worked to uphold a high ethical standard in business, fishing, and life, but also believed that if you weren't striving to get better every day you would lose your edge.

Out of that drive for excellence the East/West Tournament was born, by most accounts in the early 1990s. Initially the boats that tied up on the east side of the center fished against the boats on the west side in a daily tournament. Every day at 3 p.m., lines-out time, the captains called their daily catches in to a committee boat, which kept a running tally throughout the season. In the fall, the crews attended an East/West Banquet, where the crews learned which side won the competition and the most productive boat of the year was recognized.

"When you fish out of Oregon Inlet, it's a daily tournament," Briggs said. "Regardless of how many friends you have there, when you untie the lines you're still going to do the best you can. If you can be the top boat for the year that's a big deal. That's something you could crow about if you were a crower."

The competition still goes on today, although at some point the number of charter boats on the two sides of the marina became unbalanced, so now each team has a captain who "drafts" captains to their team at the beginning of the season. The daily battles are still intense, the banquet is still held each fall, and the trash talking is still a constant soundtrack for the veteran Oregon Inlet captains who know that to be the best in any given season at Oregon Inlet is to be among the best in the world.

Invoice for the cost of wood to build the first *Albatross* in 1935

The Foster Family:
The *Albatross* Fleet

The Tommy Gifford Award is a prestigious recognition given by the International Game Fish Association to captains and crew members who have made exceptional contributions to the world of gamefishing. Since the award's inception in 2011, sixty-four Gifford Awards have been given. Sixty-three of those recognized were individuals, and one was a pair of brothers. But only one time, in 2018, was the honor given to an entire family—the Foster family of Hatteras.

It's hard to envision where the sportfishing industry of the Outer Banks would be without the luminaries surnamed Foster who have scoured the offshore waters on boats called the *Albatross* for more than eight decades. Starting with Ernal's first attempts to hire out the new *Albatross I* to charter parties in 1937 ($15 for a full day and $10 for a half day), at least one Foster has been connected with most of the major fishing milestones out of Hatteras Inlet ever since.

In an article Michael Graff wrote for *Our State* in 2013, entitled "The Men Who Reinvented Fishing," he states, "Capt. Ernal was the first person in the state, and maybe the first on the East Coast, to take people fishing and charge them for it. Locals laughed at him. fishing for enjoyment? But what he started became an industry that changed the way people though of fishing forever."

Ernal's fledgling success at this revolutionary fishing-as-recreation venture attracted the attention of his brother Bill, who started out as his brother's mate and soon took charge of *Albatross II* when its construction was completed in 1948. In the country's recreational boom after World War II, they soon had far more interest in their charter service than they could accommodate, so in 1953 they introduced the *Albatross III* to the fleet and enlisted their cousin Milton Meekins as its captain. When Meekins died a year later, Oliver O'Neal took the helm of the *Albatross III* and ran the boat for a quarter of a century.

In a period of seven years in the fifties, both Ernal and Bill were in the cockpit of their *Albatross* crafts when charter customers caught record-breaking blue marlin. Those incredible feats, the word of which spread up and down the eastern seaboard thanks to Aycock Brown's energetic publicity efforts, helped put Hatteras on the map as a village, even if impressive hauls of cobia and dolphin were far more common than quarter-ton marlin catches.

Like their fathers before them, the second generation of sportfishing Fosters couldn't wait to start working on the family's boats themselves. Ernie had been going out on his father's boat since he was three, but at the age of fourteen he officially became a mate. Then his cousin Willy, Bill's son, became a mate himself in the late 1960s. Ernie went to North Carolina State University with plans to become an engineer, but as he put it, "I was so good in arithmetic that it only took a semester to figure out that you couldn't get much fishing done with a two-week vacation." He switched his major to education, becoming first a science teacher and then a school counselor. During his summer breaks, he continued to run charters, and he was still taking groups out on the *Albatross* boats and serving as the unofficial historian of the storied fleet years after he retired from Manteo High School.

Today the *Albatross* fleet, which they describe on their website as "the last of the traditional wooden working boats that were once found throughout the North Carolina coast," is still bringing vacationers out for unforgettable fishing days. The crews of the vessels aren't all in the Foster family anymore, but the *Albatross III* captain Sumner Mattingly is the son of the *Albatross II* captain Bryan Mattingly—an apt tribute to the spirit of family that has always inhabited the fleet that the Fosters built. Now a full day offshore is $1,600, a far cry from when Capt. Ernal hung out his shingle advertising $25 trips eighty-six years ago. The fleet's website lists nineteen different species of fish that parties might reel in, depending on the time of year they book and the type of water they choose to fish in, ranging from marlin and bluefin tuna to amberjack and Spanish mackerel.

Ernal Foster left school after the eighth grade to start his pursuit of a life on the water, but he had always been taken with the 1798 Samuel Taylor Coleridge poem, "The Rime of the Ancient Mariner." The epic work, which describes the misfortune that befalls a seaman after he kills an albatross that had led the vessel out of a storm, established the albatross as a symbol of fair seas and good fortune offshore.

As the fleet run by the Foster family increased from one to three and carried repeat charter customers on their pilgrimages to Hatteras, the talisman of the albatross has held true on this small island. As long as the Fosters' legacy is sustained and boats with "Albatross" painted on their side are heading out to sea, tight lines and full nets seem to be the norm, even eighty-five years since Ernal guided that first client out into the deep.

Postcard photo of the Oregon Inlet Fishing Center in the 1960s

CHAPTER 6

The Oregon Inlet Way

As word spread about the successful charter fleet operating out of Oregon Inlet, the most established captains were soon booked solid all the time, finding it necessary to pass parties off to other boats in the marina. Omie Tillett was one captain who had more business than he could handle, and Willie Etheridge remembers his father, Will Etheridge, taking out five charters in a single day on more than one occasion.

Naturally, such brisk demand led to the establishment of new charter boats at Oregon Inlet, especially as a new generation of sportfisherman—anglers often raised on their own father's boats—grew old enough to try the trade for themselves. Like Ernie Foster down on Hatteras Island, the second generation of charter boat captains on the northern Outer Banks benefited from the legendary pioneers who, working together, learned how to execute any task necessary to keep a boat operating and provide a successful experience for their charters.

Stories abound of early legends like Omie Tillett taking parties out for a fishing day by himself with the blessing of his father, who owned the boat. Boys not yet in their teens had already spent so much time on the water that they could capably guide a trip—even if some could hardly reach the controls. Tony Tillett loved to tell a story about the time he was eleven and guiding a trip with a twelve-year-old friend serving as mate. The customers came to the dock and kept asking each other, "Where's the captain?"

Charles Perry grew up on the boats owned by his father Charlie and his uncle Herbert, learning first from them and, when he became a mate in his teens, from Capt. Murray Cudworth and Capt. Tony Tillett. In his early days Perry was anxious to fish offshore, but his father and uncle ran most of their charters in the inlet. When his first jobs with Tillett and Cudworth finally allowed him a ride to the Gulf Stream, his mentors coached him daily, whether it was Cudworth challenging him to keep up with their route on the way out and making him navigate the boat back to shore or Tillett instructing him on the little things that would earn him more generous tips from the charters. Part of a fishing family from the cradle, Perry never wanted to do anything else, his wanderlust eventually leading him to exotic fishing adventures on every continent.

Like Perry, Willie Etheridge never played Little League Baseball or did any of the other things other boys of his age did in their free time, because from the age of eight he was on his father's charter boat. At the time he was bitter about it, wishing for a baseball glove rather than a fishing rod, but decades later he looked back on those years and appreciated his front-row seat to Outer Banks fishing history. He couldn't have understood it as a young boy, but his father was an Oregon Inlet legend; on more than one occasion when someone asked Omie Tillett to name the best fisherman he had ever seen he answered without hesitation, "Capt. Will Etheridge."

When Little Willie, as the third Will Etheridge is called, was eight or nine years old, he remembers his father Willie Jr. pulling two fence posts out of the ground and fashioning them into teasers for his charter boat, the *Chee Chee*. It was incomprehensible to Willie to attach anything to a fishing rig that didn't have a hook on it, but on the first day they tried the teasers a marlin set upon one of them. Little Willie, who runs a commercial fishing business in Wanchese, still has one of those old homemade teasers on a shelf in his office.

In the mid-1950s, around the same time his dad made those teasers, Willie Jr. became the talk of the Outer Banks when he went out and caught five giant bluefish in one day. The big blues hadn't been seen in the area in more than fifteen years, since the day in 1939 when Sam Tillett told a story about an extraordinary day of hunting for big bluefish near the coast. "When my father caught five of those bluefish it was more newsworthy than if he had caught five blue marlin," Little Willie said. "Sambo said, 'I never thought I would see them again.' He said they had been so thick in 1939 that he took a pitchfork, put on a pair of hip boots, walked out into the ocean and filled up his truck, just flipping them up on the beach."

Little Willie also has a photo of the day his father, Omie Tillett, and Moon Tillett took out a client from Norfolk—a man dressed in a suit for a day of fishing—and caught forty-two drum. It was 1953, just a year before North Carolina passed a law that no boat could take more than two drum in a day. But Capt. Willie Jr.'s legend really exploded around Oregon Inlet the day he and Little Willie caught two blue marlin on a single trip.

It was the late 1950s, so Little Willie was about eleven years old that day when he mated for his dad on an offshore charter trip. No one had ever boated two blues on one day in that area or even thought it could be done, he said. They set out their baits that morning; Capt. Willie Jr. liked to use sea mullets, and someone had given him eight or ten to take out that day. Not long after they put out a line rigged with a mullet, a blue marlin hit on it. In less than an hour and half, Willie Jr. and his party had harpooned the

285-pound fish (this was in the era before flying gaffs had been introduced to sportfishing) and brought it into the boat. But the day's drama was just beginning.

After the captain and his client, both with considerable effort, managed to extract the harpoon dart from the marlin, they reset the rig with more sea mullets and set back out. It was still only 11 a.m. when the second blue took a bait, but this time the crew was in for an epic struggle. They could tell they had a huge creature on the line, one with plenty of fight in her, and the battle to reel her in lasted nine long hours. Capt. Willie Jr. was needed to handle the line, so Little Willie, a self-described skinny, timid kid prone to seasickness, had to drive the boat. He was too short to reach the gearshift from a seated position, so he had to stay on his knees for hours in the bridge. Stepping away to go to the bathroom wasn't an option, so when he hollered out, "Daddy, I have got to pee," his father brought him a ten-quart water bucket, reminding him, "Don't you leave that throttle or that control."

Finally, as darkness fell over the Atlantic, they harpooned the second marlin and brought her on board, only to realize that they hadn't only been wrestling with a big marlin all day. They had also been in a tug of war with the sharks, who had made a feast out of the fish. "That would have been a world record marlin at that time," Willie said. "The sharks had eaten all of one side, much out of the other side and all of the guts, and it weighed 325 pounds. The record at that time was 685. We figured it was a 750, 800-pound fish."

By the time the *Chee Chee* pulled up to the fishing center word had spread about the unprecedented double-marlin day, so a large crowd was gathered around the docks to see Capt. Willie Jr. and his haul. Little Willie didn't get home until close to 1 a.m., when he fell into bed—only to be roused by his father at 4 a.m. the next morning to go out again with the same fishing party as the day before.

Willie Jr.'s reputation as a prolific catcher of fish meant that every other captain wanted to equal or exceed his success. The charter captains at Oregon Inlet always kept track of the fish they caught throughout the season, and Little Willie remembers that in 1961, Billy Baum was one billfish ahead of his father by Labor Day weekend. Capt. Willie Jr. couldn't stand being in second place, so we went out and caught two more marlin later in September, something that was unheard of at the time. At the top of his game, though, he traded in his charter business for commercial fishing, giving his son another source of incredible fish stories.

In the summer of 1962, Willie Jr. set out from Wanchese with his father on the maiden voyage of his new commercial fishing vessel. They left in late morning, intending to get in position to place their longlines after dark. The Etheridges had never been longlining before, but they knew it was a night-time pursuit. Their plans were foiled the first night, however, by fifteen-mile-per-hour northeast winds. They decided to sleep on the boat and wait it out until the next night, but when they got up the next morning they connected with an angler on the radio who said he was catching swordfish off of Cape May.

Capt. Willie Jr. turned the boat in that direction, and when they got to the right area he told Little Willie to climb to the top of the mast to look for swordfish, hoping to spend the daylight hours catching swordfish by harpoon. Little Willie was scared of heights, but he shimmied up anyway, and he was well-rewarded. "We saw sixty-two while I was up there, and they tried to spear at least ten or twelve of them but didn't get any," he said. "I'm still up the mast, holding on with both hands, excited to see the fish but scared to death of heights." That night they set up the longline, and soon Capt. Willie Jr. was the talk of the coastline as a commercial fisherman, too. Just two years after that initial longlining adventure, he set 285 hooks on a longline and caught more than 200 swordfish in one night. That catch, with its profit of more than $10,000, got Willie Jr. on his feet and allowed him to invest in his commercial business in earnest.

The members of Oregon Inlet's second generation learned the ins and outs of catching fish off the Outer Banks the way other children learn to walk, but other eager young mates found their way to the fishing center even without a family connection.

Mike Merritt was eighteen when he started working as a mate for Capt. Dan Lewark out of Wanchese, North Carolina, a facility with just seven or eight boat slips that Merritt described as more of a ditch than a marina. It was 1963, and parties paid $90 a day to book a charter, of which Merritt would receive $15 a day plus tips.

Merritt's father had served in the Coast Guard and loved the water, but he never worked as a charter boat captain, instead renting charters himself to enjoy a day of fishing and introduce the open waters to his son. The first boat Mike and his dad chartered was a legendary round-stern craft called the *Ranger,* owned by Les and Griz Evans. Even before he was hired, Merritt remembers hanging out with his father and a group of local captains in Sam and Omie's after a long fishing day. For young would-be captains like Merritt, it was an experience akin to Jack Nicklaus, new to the PGA tour, sitting around the clubhouse listening to Sam Snead and Ben Hogan spin tales from the links.

Sam and Omie's might have been best known for breakfast, but the establishment, which the Tilletts sold to Tom McKinley in the 1960s, was also a favorite evening beer-drinking spot for captains, crew members, and others to unwind. It wasn't uncommon for McKinley to go upstairs to bed, toss the keys to one of the regulars, and say, "When ya'll are done lock her up," according to Merritt.

That community of captains—characterized by authenticity, generosity, and an underlying spirit of competitiveness—served as mentors and friends to Merritt and the others who joined the burgeoning fleet in the 1960s and 1970s. It wasn't long before Merritt moved from Wanchese to Oregon Inlet, and as he made more connections at the fishing center he was struck by the deep knowledge of the captains and their willingness to share that expertise to create a better fishing experience for everyone.

"I may be biased, but I think that this particular place right here is the most phenomenal fishery and phenomenal bunch of men ever," Merritt said. "I've been offshore with people who come from other places and they say, 'I can't believe you went on the radio and told the other captains that you had all these dolphins over here.' I tell them that I know they'll do the same thing for me."

That spark of kindness and cooperation originated with Sam Tillett and was fanned into flame by his sons Omie and Tony, Charles Perry said. The result, especially in the days when fishing technology was still primitive and mastery of the various fisheries came through trial-and-error and practice, was the development of an extraordinary fleet. Through depth of experience, Outer Banks captains became known for their ability to catch anything. "If they go out there and they can't find a dolphin, then they catch tuna," Perry said. "If they can't catch tuna, they fish for wahoo. They find some way to fish and they work together. They're competitive but they work together. It's one of the best fishing spots I've ever seen."

This fraternity of captains, the key players in Oregon Inlet's rich history, include the likes of Tony Tillett and Dickie Harris who have been fishing out of the marina for over sixty years and still take charters out today. The all-important Oregon Inlet, the only outlet to the Atlantic Ocean between Virginia and Hatteras, has been one of the key catalysts in the emergence of the Outer Banks as a fishing destination. It has enabled countless memorable offshore trips and inspired some of the East Coast's most prolific boatbuilders. But the history of the inlet itself is complicated and, at times, tragic. This channel, linked to the livelihood of many people and the recreational pursuits of even more, is bound to the whims of the volatile coastal weather that formed it in the first place.

When a ferocious hurricane slammed the Outer Banks in 1846, the intense winds did considerable damage but also created Oregon Inlet. As Merlin S. Berry explained in his book *History of Northeastern North Carolina Storms*, "A remarkable surge of water, driven by continuous northeast winds, pushed far into the Pamlico and Albemarle sounds, flooding rivers and creeks for miles inland. Then, as the hurricane passed and its winds rotated to the southwest, this massive expanse of water rushed back toward the sea, overwashing the Outer Banks from west to east."

Legend has it that the first vessel to pass through the new inlet, albeit inadvertently, was a ship called *Oregon* struggling through that violent storm en route from Edenton, North Carolina to Bermuda. A huge wave lifted the embattled boat onto a sandbar, giving the crew a reprieve while the storm cleared. When they could get their bearings, they found a huge cut in the island that allowed them to pass back out into the ocean. The vessel lent its name to the inlet, some thirteen years before a northwestern territory of the same name became one of the United States.

From that tumultuous beginning, the inlet has been the subject of triumphs like the construction of the Bonner Bridge, countless political clashes, and periodic disasters. In 1960 alone seven people died in three separate accidents in the inlet, which is subject to constantly shifting sidebars and is particularly hazardous in an east or northeast wind. In 1968 a dredge trying to clear the inlet ran aground, and in 1982 winter storms in the area caused such severe shoaling that the inlet was closed to all but the smallest boats for two weeks. In 1970 Congress approved a major improvement project to build jetties and deepen the channel, but concerns about environmental impact and cost stalled the bill which, remarkably, is still being debated by lawmakers more than fifty years later. In August 2022 Rep. Greg Murphy (R.-N.C) introduced new legislation that would construct a dual jetty system to stabilize the inlet.

Whether the proposed solution is jetties, more regular dredging, or adapted navigational routes through the inlet, it has prompted much debate and consternation almost since the day that a hurricane formed it. In 1961, the North Carolina Wildlife Resources Commission called it the most hazardous place for boaters in the entire state, and two generations later, in a 2007 *Salt Water Sportsman* article, a retired Coast Guardsman named Dan Willard called it "one of the most dangerous places on the East Coast," estimating that five or six recreational boats a year capsize in the inlet.

With every year of growth in the Outer Banks' maritime landscape, captains, boatbuilders, crew members, and avid recreational anglers learn more about the water and the conditions that come to bear on it. Computerized design and navigational technology have eliminated many of question marks that characterized early forays offshore. But the ongoing travails surrounding Oregon Inlet are an apt reminder that the the sea, along with its channels and coastlines, is still an untamed environment, as unpredictable as the creatures that live in its depths.

From figuring out how to navigate the inlet safely to trying out new tackle or drafting new boats designs to respond to the area's specific conditions, necessity sparked ingenuity at Oregon Inlet. Soon this close-knit fishing community was populated with all manner of experts ready to guide and equip visitors and captains alike. It was a fully functional, self-sufficient society that could provide an exceptional fishing experience without any outside resources. Many satisfied charter customers came away with an impressive haul of dolphin, a sailfish, or even a blue marlin. Others, like Jack Herrington of Allison Park, Pennsylvania, went on a fishing expedition off of Oregon Inlet and made history.

The date was July 26, 1974, and Herrington had chartered a trip with Capt. Harry Baum on board the *Jo-Boy*. The craft was thirty-nine miles east-southeast of Oregon Inlet when, at about 10:30 a.m., a giant fish hit the double-hooked mullet on Herrington's line—prompting the crew, including Harry Baum and his mate Richard Baum, to jump into action to help him wrestle the massive fish into the boat. It was a Herculean effort, requiring extra men from a nearby boat, to land the first blue marlin Herrington had ever caught, a world-record-breaking 1,142 pounds.

When Herrington first spotted the marlin jumping above the waves, he told a reporter shortly after the catch that he thought it looked more like a whale than anything. "He fought for nearly three hours—the crew using water to cool the reel, his body aching and sweat running down his face—before he reeled the beast to the boat," read a 2018 *Virginian-Pilot* article about the accomplishment. In a 1997 *Greensboro News and Record* article Herrington recounted his most memorable day on the water:

"It jumped more times than we could count," Herrington said. "We had it on 100-pound-test line with a 9/0 Penn reel. The captain did a heck of a job with the boat. But we had to get some folks off a nearby boat, the *Duchess of Dare*, to help us get it into the *Jo-Boy*. Took seven of us all together. The scales couldn't weigh it at the [Oregon Inlet] Fishing Center, so we loaded it into a truck and took it to the Hatteras Marlin Club."

At the time, Herrington's fish outweighed the previous world record holder by a whopping 300 pounds, but three years later the record was broken with a 1,157-pound blue off the coast of Madeira. The Oregon Inlet catch, the first grander ever brought in off the North Carolina coast, stood as a state record for thirty-four years. Just a year later in 1975, though, the Hatteras fleet came close to that state record when the *Jersey Devil*, guided by Capt. Ronnie Jones, brought in a 1,128-pound blue marlin with angler Fulton Katz in the chair.

When Herrington died in 2018, his relatives donated his extraordinary fish to the Graveyard of the Atlantic Museum on Hatteras Island. It's a monument not only to the angler, says Mike Merritt, but also to Capt. Harry Baum, who facilitated the historic event with equipment that most would consider insufficient for the task. "That was the greatest feat for catching a blue marlin," Merritt said. "He caught this 1,142-pound blue on a 9-aught reel, a black-sided one, with star drag. The drag was sketchy to say the least, he probably didn't have 300 yards of 100-pound monofilament, and the guides on the rod had vinyl tape around them. It was incredible."

A grander caught off of Oregon Inlet inspired the hopes of anglers everywhere along the East Coast, and even though Aycock Brown was nearing seventy he was still sending photos to every newspaper he could find and carefully ensuring that catches like Herrington's earned their rightful place in the record books. Brown didn't waste any time in heralding his county's accomplishments, as evidenced by the fact that a Mr. Elwood K. Harry from the International Game Fish Association (IGFA) wrote him a letter just three days after Herrington's feat requesting thorough documentation. "We would appreciate any information and photographs that you could furnish on this catch, as this could very well be the marlin over 1,000 pounds that so many anglers have been seeking over the past year," Harry wrote.

Before long the IGFA was satisfied that Oregon Inlet had in fact been the site of an enormous marlin catch, and for Capt. Harry Baum what started out as an ordinary charter trip had become a story that no one would ever tire of hearing. His gear might not have been state-of-the-art, but his fishing expertise, sharpened in that extraordinary community of captains, was enough to put the Outer Banks even more indelibly on the map.

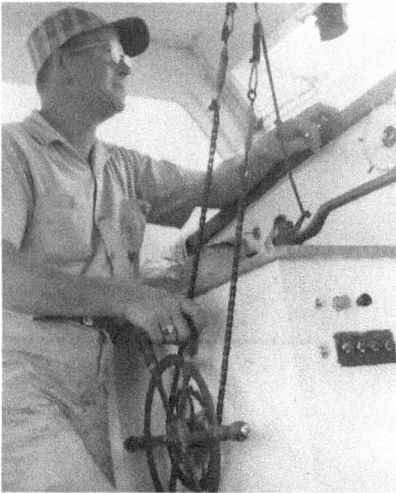

Capt. Lee Perry in his youth
with early bridge steering, 1955

Capt. Billy Baum ("The Baumer")
with the fisherman's stare, 1959

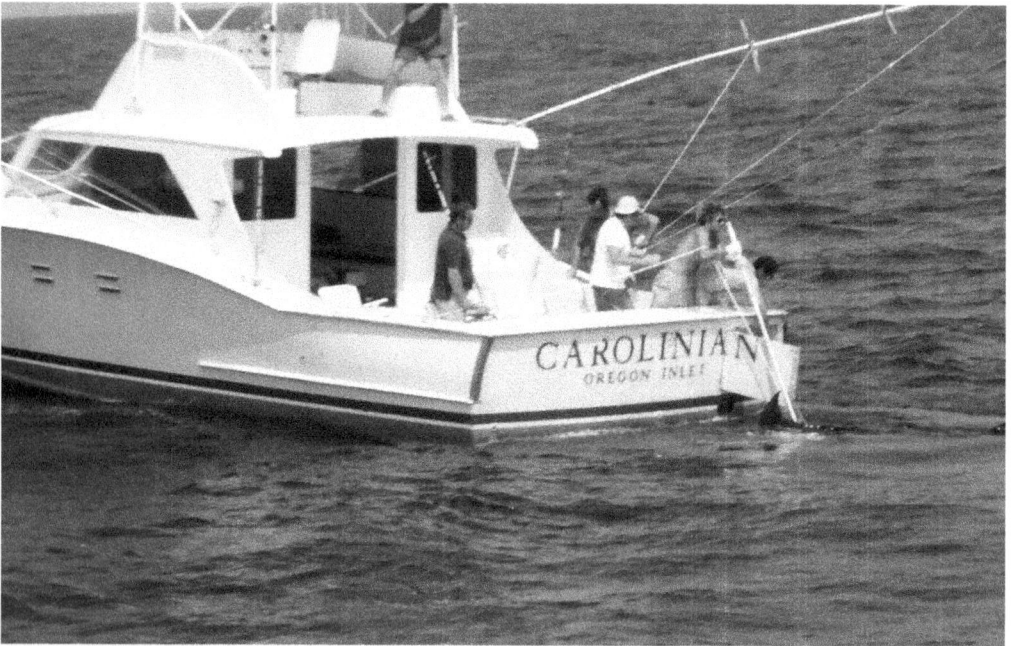

Capt. Tony Tillett pulling blue marlin through the tuna door on the *Carolinian*, 1960s

Capt. Murray Cudworth and mate Charles Perry weighing in a blue marlin at Oregon Inlet, 1961

Teenage Charles Perry unloading the fish box, a daily routine, 1963

The *Sportsman*, Capt. Omie Tillett's first boat, 1961

Crowd gathering to watch weigh-in at Hatteras Marlin Club, 1970s

Brothers Tony (left) and Omie (right) Tillett with blue marlin catch, 1972

Weighing in a big blue marlin at Hatteras Marlin Club, 1970s

Hang 'em high, 1973

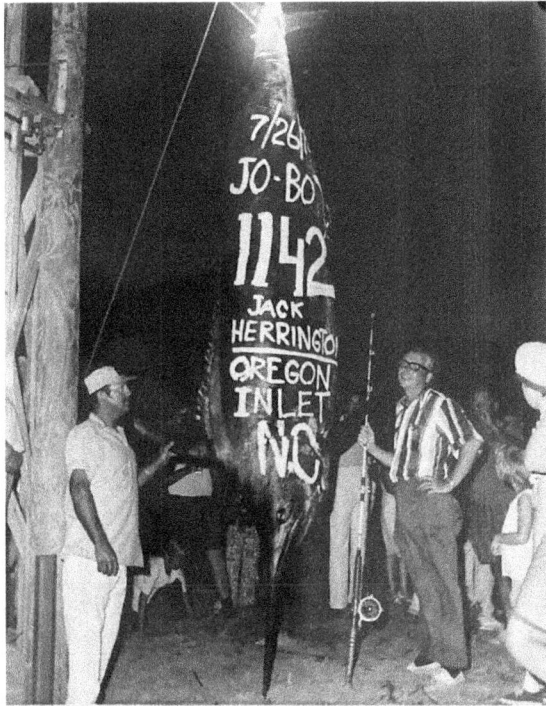

Capt. Harry Baum (left) world record, 1974

Aycock Brown (right) giving photography tips to Charles Perry, 1975

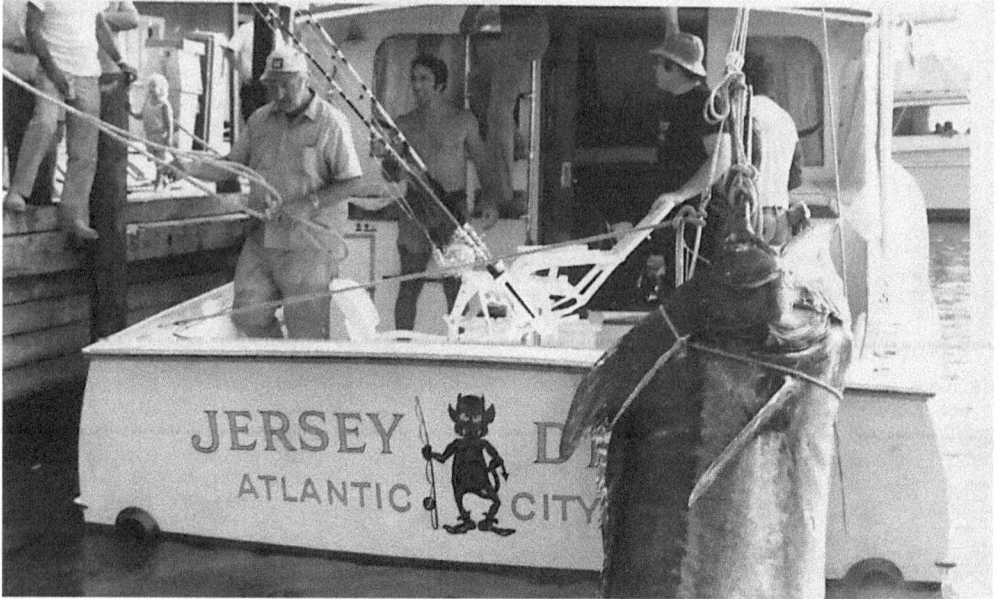

Capt. Ronnie Jones towed a grander in that wouldn't fit through the door in Hatteras, 1975.

Capt. Lee Perry kneeling on the left, 1980s

Charles Perry with Capt. Omie Tillett, 1980s

Capt. Omie Tillett portrait, 1980s

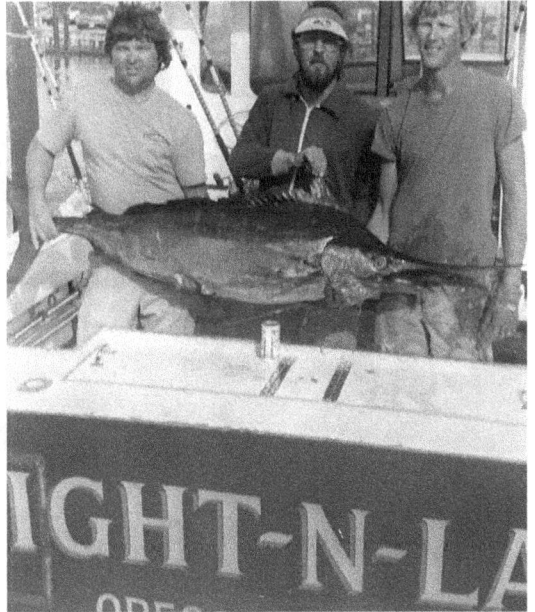

Capt. Sam Stokes, Kenny Jo, Capt. John Bayliss left to right on the Fight-N-Lady, 1980s

Second boat Capt. Sam Stokes ran en route from Buddy Davis' boatyard in Wanchese to be launched, 1980s

Blue marlin right before the bite, 1990s

Capt. Sunny Briggs (middle) and mate Buddy Davis (right) with a charter on the *Jerry Jr.* in 1967. Nice bull dolphin!

CHAPTER 7

Trial, Error, and Innovation

In their early days building boats together in Manteo, Sunny Briggs and Paul Mann used to joke that they should call their enterprise T&E Boatworks—because the process of crafting a seaworthy, effective fishing boat hinged on countless hours of trial and error. Briggs and Mann are part of a unique generation of boatbuilders on the Outer Banks; they weren't the earliest pioneers, but they were the ones who saw the techniques, materials, and designs change the most dramatically during their time in the business.

"In my era of boatbuilding, I was involved in the greatest amount of change and growth," said Mann, who retired in 2021 after building more than forty custom hulls. "In my era we went through the biggest change in sportfishing history in terms of the boats, from what they were to what they are today."

In a sense, Briggs, Mann and their counterparts represent the bridge between trailblazers like Warren O'Neal, Omie Tillett, Buddy Cannady, Billy Baum, and Buddy Davis and the custom-focused, technology-driven boatbuilding enterprises of today. They understand that progress has driven change over the decades and they appreciate many of the latest cutting-edge advancements, but they can't help but pine for the days when a boatbuilder was part designer, part mechanic, part carpenter, and part steering engineer.

"We had to learn how to build a boat from beginning to end whether we liked it or not," Mann said. "We couldn't specialize. Nobody could specialize. You weren't pigeonholed. I set up the jigs, I did mechanical, I did electrical, you had to do it all. You were just working. And I learned how to build a boat from the design stage to the go-fishing stage, every aspect of it—from the designing of the hull to the building of the hull, to the fairing of the hull, to the glassing to the finish work to the interior work. We learned it all, from the very basic design all the way to the finished product."

Like so many of his Oregon Inlet counterparts, Mann grew up on the water, working as a mate for the first time as a teenager and earning his captain's license at the age of twenty. He learned the charter fishing trade, but he had a hand in boatbuilding through every stage of his life as well—watching Warren O'Neal build boats in Manteo when he was a young boy because O'Neal and his father were good friends. He learned the ins and outs of the craft by working with Briggs and others, and when he was twenty-eight he built his first sportfishing boat for his own use—a 52-footer called the *Madd Hatter*.

Mann knew all of the best early boatbuilders and had helped out in many of their shops, but the designs that inspired him the most were those of Buddy Cannady. He believes that Cannady never got the recognition he deserved for crafting "the best running boat in the ocean." Cannady's boats were utilitarian, he said, but they were reliable and dry and they're some of the best all-around performers in any fleet to this day. In a classic example of the generational knowledge that has accumulated to create a boatbuilding juggernaut on the Northern Outer Banks, Cannady learned some of his most effective techniques for the bottoms of his boats from Ricky Scarborough, whose work as a commercial crabber and a duck hunting guide in the 1960s led him first to specialize in boats suited to those pursuits.

Scarborough initially taught himself to build the flat-bottomed skiffs best suited to crabbing, and he also crafted a 17-foot tunnel boat to help him guide duck hunting parties through shallow water. His friends from the Duck Island Club and others who hunted on the Outer Banks were so impressed with his skiffs that he could hardly keep up with the demand. He built more than 100 skiffs for customers before pivoting to sportfishing boats in the 1970s after learning the finer points of custom boatbuilding from—who else?—Omie Tillett. Scarborough died in 2020; his son Ricky Jr. is carrying on his tradition of excellence at the helm of Scarborough Boatworks, the company his father founded in 1977.

When Mann resolved to build the boat that became the *Madd Hatter* in 1988, he tried to pull the best tips and tricks from Briggs, Cannady, Scarborough, and Bobby Sullivan, but Sullivan offered more than boatbuilding inspiration. Mann had assisted Sullivan, who had learned from Allen Hayman and then taken over his mentor's Point Harbor workshop. In 1986, when Sullivan started work on his second charter boat, *Marlin Fever,* he asked Mann to assist him. The next year, Sullivan offered the same workshop for Mann's use when the younger builder started work on the *Madd Hatter.*

"I started with a block plane, a hammer, and the will and energy that no one could tell me I couldn't do something," Mann told *Power and Motor Yacht* in a 2021 article. "I willed myself through all this and I was never so arrogant to think I couldn't learn. I learned from everybody."

His fellow captains admired the *Madd Hatter* and started placing orders for boats of their own. So for a time Mann took out fishing parties seven days a week during the warm months and worked in his own Manns Harbor boatbuilding shop, which he constructed in seven days in 1988, for six days a week when it was cooler. As one of the youngest builders along the coast, he was underestimated at first, but his boats performed so well offshore that he didn't need official advertising to soon find himself with more orders than he could handle. After a few years of nonstop work at sea and in his shop, Mann quit his charter business and made Mann Boatworks a full-time pursuit.

Mann was always meticulous about planning his boats, and whenever a new technique came along he didn't adopt it just because it seemed like the latest and greatest idea. Instead, he tested every innovation thoroughly before he decided to adopt it on his boats. He was guided by voices like that of Billy Baum, the legendary captain and boatbuilder in the 1960s who used to tell Mann, "You've got to make it round to make it straight." It was a bit of advice that confounded Mann when he was young, but he came to understand that Baum was talking about convexity, or what Baum called "delta conic," on the boat's bottom, a unique rounded design that helped a craft perform better in rough seas. It's a hull that is ubiquitous today, but Baum was one of its pioneers, and Mann was an apprentice watching innovators like Baum tinker until they achieved the type of performance that could offer both a smooth ride and a fruitful fishing outing.

For his first twenty years as a boatbuilder Mann used the plank-on-frame technique to shape his boats, which is a practice that is now obsolete with the prevalence of jig boats, or those with a preformed mold of the hull that allows the work to be done upside down. Before he turned out his first jig boat, the *Qualifier*, in 2009, Mann adhered to the tried-and-true method, but that doesn't mean he rejected innovation. He believes he was the only boatbuilder to incorporate convexity into plank-on-frame hulls, and he was also an early adopter of flipping his plank-on-frame boats over for the glassing and fairing processes, which saved money on construction and made tasks easier for his employees.

Another trend that significantly changed the game for Mann and his contemporaries was the surge in horsepower, with a once-incredible capacity of 1,000 horsepower leading to engines that could pull close to 2,000 horsepower just a few years later. The boat engine companies, like Caterpillar and GM Diesel, would sometimes fly Mann and other prominent boatbuilders to see the new machines as they came off the line. He still remembers his disbelief when he witnessed his first 1,000-horsepower engine, and then his astonishment when, on the same trip, the engineers said they could double that power on the same engine block.

For a boatbuilder trying to keep pace with such rapid progress, Mann had to work with each customer to determine their distinct priorities. For instance, as bigger engines led to faster running speeds, adaptations to the hull became more essential. "You can go really fast in a boat on the water if you can keep the boat glued to the water," Mann said. "When they start coming out of the water that's when you're getting ready to tear something up. As we got more power and speed, breaking the forty-knot barrier, we had to learn how to keep 'em glued to the water."

Mann became a student of the necessary compromises of boat-building, whether it was prioritizing design elements that can make a boat run more smoothly in choppy waters or focusing on creating the best fishing craft, albeit one that might not offer the smoothest ride out to the Gulf Stream. "Do you want to go a little slower and be really comfortable for eight hours of fishing, or do you want to get there thirty minutes sooner and then roll like a biscuit?" Mann said. "That is the truth of a matter. You can build a great fishing platform or you can build a great running boat. I don't think there's any such thing as a perfect boat, but you can make it better all the way around."

Mann made one such adjustment when he designed the 56-footer called the *Pelican* in the late 1990s for Arch Bracher. It was a priority for Bracher to be able to go out when conditions were choppy, so he and Mann sat down and designed a hull with a little more midrise and a sharper forward. Bracher knew that his boat would burn a little more fuel and go a little slower than some of the other boats in the fleet, but it would have the smooth ride he desired. Another tweak Mann made was for a client in Aruba, who needed a boat that would run hard in a head sea. Today that Paul Mann craft is one of the smoothest in the Caribbean; the other boats get behind it to come in when conditions are rough.

Even though he's enjoying his retirement and he knew the time was right when he stepped away, Mann misses the challenge of solving problems, of creating the optimal craft that is individualized to the boater or angler who comes to order it. The advancements that were just starting to emerge in the industry in Mann's later years, like vacuum bagging and resin infusion, are already standard practice today, and he looks on with amazement as new materials and techniques for building boats, aided by the type of technology no one could have even imagined when he started building in the 1980s, seem to emerge almost daily.

Sunny Briggs, one of Mann's earliest and most important mentors and the person who modeled that "trial-and-error" approach in the shop, constructed more than sixty boats between thirty-five and seventy feet in his career. When he "retired" in his late 1970s he promptly built a huge shop in his backyard so that he could keep building boats for friends and family. Even though he started earlier than Mann, he was also swept along in the era of brisk progress that seemed to put forth another new material or technique as soon as a builder had learned the particulars of the last innovation.

Briggs and his boats are known up and down the Outer Banks for their dependable designs and sound construction; as he told *Marlin* magazine in 2021, "You really cannot cut corners or take shortcuts when you're striving for greatness." A key reason for Briggs' reputation as an industry pioneer is the fact that he was the first in the area to use CNC technology in boatbuilding. CNC, which stands for "Computer Numerical Control," uses computer-generated designs to plan and cut the parts of a boat, ensuring uniformity and reducing waste. In the 1980s, when Briggs first considered the idea of CNC for boat construction, the machines had been around for decades but were used primarily in other types of manufacturing. It was actually his wife Dee who broached the idea. She was working in the furniture business, where CNC technology was commonplace, and she asked Sunny what he thought of incorporating the machines into his boatbuilding operation.

At that time, a Florida builder named Steve French was designing Briggs' hulls, so Sunny asked him what he thought of Dee's proposal. "We called him at about 8 p.m. one night, and I said, 'Steve, Dee has a harebrained idea, and I want you to listen to it,'" Briggs said. As he recalls, French replied by saying, "I've built over 1,000 boats, and what she's asking you to do has never been done before. Give me two days."

Two days later French called back and said he thought it would work. They invested in a CNC machine, which standardized the process by cutting all of the boat parts to French's specifications after he entered his designs into the computer. That was the mid-1980s, and it took a few years before it dawned on the other top area boatbuilders that Briggs had modernized his process with a secret weapon. When they asked him what made his boats different, he told them, driven by that spirit of generosity and friendly competitiveness that Omie Tillett had sown in him years earlier. And just a few years after they introduced CNC at Briggs Boatworks, French started his own company, French Yachts, out of Stuart, Florida, touting the CNC cutting technology as a key selling point. Today, up and down the east coast, every significant boatbuilding operation is using CNC to cut out its boats.

Not every innovator on the Outer Banks was actually building boats. Some, like Billy McCaskill, saw a rise in demand for the key components on a sportfishing boat and brought their own sportfishing experience to bear on pursuits like engine repair and the production of new gear and tackle. Those who were actually out on the water every day had the ideal vantage point to understand what was needed to make fishing more efficient and fruitful, and often they had the necessary vision and skill, when they got back on land, to create that better piece of gear or incorporate a new element of boat design.

Like most of the men who have made a career out of the Outer Banks fishing industry, McCaskill started as a mate in his teens, working first for Sam Stokes and then for Sunny Briggs. But after several years mastering the art of baiting hooks—he used to joke that his business card should read "CEO of Mullet Management"— McCaskill tried the furniture business, a menial job planting beach grass in the sand, and even taxidermy before learning to build custom fishing rods and then opening Whalebone Tackle in Nags Head. His fishing rods were made to perform in the waters off those barrier islands, and as word got out he had trouble keeping up with the orders. He never advertised, and in his busiest winter he crafted thirty-seven custom rods.

It would be near the turn of the century before larger boatbuilding operations started to pop up on the Outer Banks, but the early foundation laid by Warren O'Neal, Omie Tillett, and their contemporaries sparked builders like Mann and Briggs to continue and add to the tradition. The advancements coming to the boatbuilding industry in the next three decades might have amazed the backyard builders and the owners of the smaller shops, but the seeds for every innovation were planted by those pioneers. Through every era, the captains and boatbuilders on the Outer Banks were driven by a dual commitment to excellence and progress.

Lee Perry (left) and Sunny Briggs (right) on the *"Deepwater,"* Lee Perry's marlin magnet, 1961

Lee Perry: "Soda Crackers All Over the Bridge!"

Not every old-timer who made a living fishing off the Outer Banks had the experience of catching a grander, or winning a major fishing tournament, or setting up in a plethora of giant bluefin tuna. But every captain, mate, or boatbuilder who spent time there in the 1950s or 1960s has at least one priceless Lee Perry story.

As the captain of the *Deepwater* for a quarter century and a fixture at the Oregon Inlet Fishing Center and in various boatbuilding shops, Perry was a character without equal along the coast. The phrases he coined, often in blustery, lisp-accented enthusiasm when he had a good bite, are still part of the everyday vernacular on the Outer Banks. Odds are excellent that a weekday lunch at Sam and Omie's will be punctuated by at least one Lee Perry tale.

Lee had a speech impediment resulting from a childhood cleft palate repair, and that characteristic, along with his tendency to talk faster when he was excited, meant that some charter clients might spend the whole day on his boat without understanding much of what he said. He also had cataracts, and to correct his vision he wore thick glasses that resembled the bottoms of Coca-Cola bottles. He was at his most animated when at the bridge of his fishing boat, said Charles Perry, who was Lee's first cousin. When he hooked a marlin or another big fish, he loved to share his enthusiasm with fellow captains over the radio, and everyone in the fleet would gather around so they wouldn't miss a syllable.

"Fishing excited him as much as anyone could get excited," Charles Perry said. "The last blue marlin he saw was just as exciting as the first blue marlin he saw, I promise you. Sometimes he would get so charged up that he forgot he was holding the mic button down on the radio. He'd talk nonstop for three or four minutes. All of us would be laughing. He was hilarious . . . We'd sit up on the bridge and listen and laugh and laugh."

It was during one such outburst that Capt. Lee coined one of his most enduring "Lee-isms." He almost always ate crackers while he steered the boat, and on one particular day, when his crew brought in a big marlin, he took to the radio to describe his reaction to the catch. "Soda crackers all over the bridge!" he shouted, thus originating one of the region's favorite descriptive phrases for a big fishing day. And as Charles Perry discovered to his delight in Costa Rica in 2021, the expression isn't limited to the Outer Banks; he couldn't believe his ears when he heard a stranger over the radio exclaim, "Soda crackers all over the bridge!"

If a young angler was going to sign on as Lee's mate he needed to come in with a healthy self-esteem, since Lee was known for withering criticisms of mates on slow fishing days. Mike Merritt remembers walking out to Lee's boat at the fishing center one day and overhearing Lee telling a charter client that he wouldn't be able to hook a marlin that day because of his mate. "He can't hook 'em!"

Lee said. "I'm not going to take you marlin fishing because the damn boy can't hook a marlin." Lee was also legendary for hiring, firing, and rehiring mates at a dizzying rate, depending on that day's results.

Sunny Briggs mated for him in his early years on the waterfront, and he learned not to take the "layoffs" too seriously. "I fished with him for five seasons, and I got fired a lot," Briggs said. "He would fire and rehire daily. Once it happened to me three times in a day. You would hook a good fish, and he would say, 'Good job, you're rehired.' " Regular charter clients got to know Lee and his idiosyncrasies, and he had a polarizing effect, Briggs said. "Lee had charters who would either fish with him once and say I'm never going to fish with him again, or they would fish with him and they didn't ever want to fish with anyone else.

"He made me a better person," Briggs said. "People say, 'How can you see someone who's bent out of shape with you, cussing and carrying on, and just look at them and smile?' And my answer is, 'I worked for Lee Perry.' I've heard it all, and it made me thick-skinned. But he was a good man. He was a unique character but he had a heart of gold, and he would help anybody."

Even if Lee was easy to mess with, the more established he got on the waterfront the more readily he would give it right back. When he reported a blue marlin catch on the radio, a fellow captain would respond by saying "shark" to get him riled up, suggesting that what he had caught wasn't really a marlin. Lee grabbed his radio and hollered, "Whoever sharked me, come on over here to my boat. I'll cut your heart out!"

Lee didn't just enliven offshore fishing trips; he also added spice to the long days spent building boats in the offseason. When he worked with Omie Tillett in Warren O'Neal's shop, Lee was on the receiving end of numerous practical jokes. He was an irresistible target for such pranks, because his reactions were unforgettable. On one particular afternoon, Lee and Omie were assisting Warren on the construction of the *Sea Byrd*. The two men were in the cabin together, doing framing work, and Omie repeatedly dropped nails in front of Lee, knowing that every time Lee hit one with his knee he would jerk up and hit his head on the ceiling in the cramped space. He also glued Lee's toolbox to the floor.

From outside the cabin, Warren heard repeated loud thuds, mixed with expletives in Lee's unmistakable voice. After a few of the thumps, Lee would crawl out, examine his nail pouch and then re-enter the cabin, when the events would start again. "Loud stammering followed the next wallop and Lee climbed out of the hull," Neal Conoley recounted in his book. "He stomped over to his workbench, removed his nail belt and reached down to pick up his toolbox. In anger, he jerked up on the toolbox but it wouldn't budge. Lee mumbled a few words, gave the box a swift kick and hobbled out of the shop."

Mike Merritt loves to retell another Lee Perry classic: the pudding story. Back then they kept the epoxy glue in big cut-off gallon milk jugs; Omie would tell everyone in the county to save their milk jugs and drop them off at his shop. When you mixed up the glue in the jug, it had a pale yellow color and looked like vanilla custard. Lee would often comment, "Omie, it looks like pudding. It looks like you could eat it."

One day a local captain named Alan Foreman was there, and he and some of the other guys went to lunch at a local deli. They passed a grocery store and saw a six-pack of Del Monte vanilla pudding in the window, which gave Foreman an idea. He bought the pudding, and when he got back he secretly dumped three of the cups into an empty epoxy jug, then grabbed the wooden stick they always used to stir the glue and walked out in front of Lee.

"You know something, Lee?" Alan said. "This stuff looks just like pudding, I declare I believe you could eat it."

"You better not eat that, boy," Lee replied.

"I believe I'll eat it."

"I'll bet you five dollars you won't do it."

When Alan put the stick full of "epoxy" in his mouth, Lee cried out, "Ohhhhh my god, you're gonna die! Omie, he's gonna die!" Then he reached into his pocket, found some crumpled bills and held them out to Alan. "Well, I've got three dollars here, but if you're still alive tomorrow I'll give you the other two!"

Lee died in 1990, but it is a certainty that his influence will be felt for generations in and around Oregon Inlet. In a county that is renowned for colorful characters, Lee elevated nonconformity to an art form without ever trying to do so. He was hilarious, gullible, and good-natured, and in his one-of-a-kind way he helped give the Outer Banks fishing culture its distinct character.

Kill Fest: A collection of well trained big fish assassins, 1973 (before tag and release became popular)

CHAPTER 8

Granders and a Bluefin Bonanza

While growing demand for slips at the Oregon Inlet Fishing Center and an explosion of boatbuilding seemed to bring a new charter operation to the northern Outer Banks every week, change was a bit slower to dawn at Hatteras Inlet, where the *Albatross* fleet and other long-time boats like the *Twins* and the *Twins II* commanded the market well into the 1970s. Up until the middle of that decade, Ernal Foster and his family had lived and worked out of a big waterfront house on the inlet, which had ample room to dock the three *Albatross* boats.

The Fosters had long been renting the house and land, but in the mid-1970s it was sold to an outside developer, pushing the Fosters out of their home and, through the subsequent development of the property to build a motel there, diminishing the land adjacent to the docks, known as Foster's Quay, which Ernal did own. Eventually Foster reached a détente with the new owners that allowed the captains better access to parking and boat slips, but the wheels of progress were about to start turning again on Hatteras Island.

In the early 1970s, a project began to widen the creek leading to Foster's Quay and dredge the area around the Hatteras Harbor Marina, which essentially rolled out the red carpet for new charter operations to move in. Buddy Hooper was a young captain in Hatteras around that time, trying to learn the ropes from legends like the Fosters and Edgar Styron. It was a conversation with Styron one day that helped shape the ethic that guided Hooper's fishing efforts for decades.

On that day Hooper had been out all morning and had ten blue marlin within striking distance. Of the ten he had seen close to his boat he had broken four off on the leader and pulled hooks on two on the leader, and he was feeling discouraged about what might have been. He came back to Hatteras and complained to Styron about his day, and Styron had a succinct reply: "Son, show me, don't tell me." The next day Hooper got up early and went out again, and that time he boated four blue marlin. "Show me, don't tell me," became a guiding principle.

The *Albatross* fleet had more competition than ever during this period, due to the expansion of marina capacity and the Aycock Brown-fueled frenzy that came on the heels of the historic 1975 blue marlin catch off Hatteras. That triumph, which took place on the Warren O'Neal boat the *Jersey Devil,* would have been the talk of the East Coast if not for the fact that Jack Herrington had caught one that weighed a scant fourteen pounds more just a year earlier on June 26, 1974 off Oregon Inlet. A New Jersey angler named Dr. Fulton Katz, supported by locals Capt. Ronnie Jones, Mike Sobel, and Edgar Styron Sr., captured their prize from the *Jersey Devil* on June 21, 1975.

Homer Styron wasn't offshore with his dad Edgar that day, but he was on the docks at the Texaco dock when the *Jersey Devil* backed in with its prize. Charles Perry was also there that day and had been fishing for big marlin in Australia for many seasons, so he had learned to spot a grander on sight. Perry saw the marlin's tail hanging down in the water because the fish was longer than the 46-foot boat's cockpit, and he hollered out to Jones, "I've seen some big fish, and this one's well over 1,000 pounds!" Jones responded, "Are you sure?" and Perry said, "Look out! That fish isn't going to make it to the dock."

Perry's prediction would soon be proved accurate, but they wouldn't learn the fish's true size at Hatteras Marlin Club. The fish was too large to fit on the scales there, and everyone knew that Herrington's marlin had been weighed at Oregon Inlet. So they put the giant in the back of a truck and motored north to the fishing center. As Perry recalled it, the fish fell apart when they hoisted it up, but they were able to get an official weight of 1,128 pounds. It might have only been the second-largest blue marlin caught off the Outer Banks within a year, but it was extraordinary nonetheless, and it helped cement the area's reputation as a big-time game fishing destination.

According to José M. Acostamadiedo, who wrote a paper for the University of Vermont called "Legendary Granders of the Outer Banks," the North Carolina barrier islands are the only place on the East Coast that has held the world Atlantic blue marlin record three different times, and it's the only area with more than one of the IGFA's top ten largest Atlantic blue marlin catches. But while captains, crews, and charter captains fervently hoped that two granders in a year portended a future pattern, that period in the mid-1970s was more an outlier than a trend. Since 1975, despite plenty of large marlin both in and out of tournament competition, only five marlin over 1,000 pounds have been caught on the Outer Banks, and like the proximity of Herrington and Katz's catches, three of those were hooked within five years of each other in the late 1980s and early 1990s. That cluster of good fishing fortune is even more extraordinary when you consider that the only grander ever caught out of nearby Beaufort Inlet was also brought in during the same period.

That particular streak of thousand-plus-pounders commenced on August 22, 1987, with Capt. Sam Stokes guiding angler Robert Senneville on Stokes's 53-footer the *Fight-N-Lady*, which was built by Omie Tillett. The crew was about fifty miles northeast of Oregon Inlet when a huge marlin hooked on a large ballyhoo and jumped eight or ten times before settling down. "We had her to the boat in an hour and forty minutes and just backed down and washed her right through the tuna (transom) door and into the cockpit. The fish was just about dead," Stokes remembered later in an interview with Bob Hutchinson of the *Greensboro News and Record*. The marlin weighed in at 1,020 pounds. An incredible picture from that tournament (shown on page 67) captures the riches the Atlantic held for the anglers who competed that year: Capt. Lee Perry standing in front of four marlin weighing 791 pounds, 958 pounds, 1,020 pounds, and 813 pounds.

A year and five days later, on August 27, 1988, another grander paid a welcome visit to the *Teaser*, skippered by Capt. Brenner Parks with angler Michael Jeffries in the fighting chair. The boat was entered in the Pirate's Cove Billfish Tournament, and they were fishing about forty miles northeast of Oregon Inlet when they hooked the fish at about 1 p.m., as Parks recalled to Acostamadiedo. "Capt. Brynner Parks spots a large fish trying to eat his bridge teaser and realizes that it has a mackerel and a leader hanging out of its mouth," Acostamadiedo wrote in his 2005 paper. "He yells to angler Mike Jeffries to crank the slack in and he throttles the boat ahead. Despite these efforts Mike Jeffries could not get the slack out. Eventually the fish decided to turn to one side and start pulling to the northeast...The fish then took on a series of short thrashing jumps in the usual fashion of large fish, when most of the body stays in the water and just the head and shoulders and belly come out of the water, churning it up. Then she settled in, and for five-and-a-half hours they were attached by a Dacron umbilical cord. Several times the leader could have been within reach but she paddled away."

Parks and his crew finally got the marlin into the boat at about 6:30 and pulled into Pirate's Cove Marina at 9 p.m. under a full moon. "We were lucky," Parks told Hutchinson. "A fish like that can find 100 ways to get free. It was spectacular. You can't believe how strong a fish like that is until you experience it." Even though Capt. John Bayliss and his *Tarheel* won that particular tournament because he accumulated more release points than Parks and Jeffries, the *Teaser's* 1,085-pound prize still hangs in the restaurant at Pirate's Cove.

Less than a year after the *Teaser's* catch, on August 12, 1989, Howard Basnight on the *Wave Runner* caught a 1,002-pound marlin while competing in the Band-The-Billfish Tournament in Morehead City. While not an Outer Banks story, Basnight's feat fits neatly in the timeline of extraordinary fish brought in within a strikingly short period. After that, it was three more years before Capt. Buckshot Piper, guiding a private boat called *Allison,* and angler Slim Flinchum reeled in a 1,021-pound blue fifty miles northeast of Oregon Inlet on August 22, 1992. The catch was in the same vicinity as those from both the *Fight-N-Lady* and the *Teaser.* It was the last Outer Banks grander of the century, and as the crew later reported, it was a dramatic conquest involving two flying gaffs, assistance from other crews, and a voluntary swim by one of his crew members.

As Flinchum told Hutchinson about that catch: "When she hit, it looked like someone had dropped a Cadillac into the water." The marlin jumped countless times and then dove deep, but Flinchum held his own in the battle," Piper said. It took less than two hours for the crew to get the marlin subdued near the boat, at which point mate Carl Spina jumped overboard to tie a rope to the fish's tail to ease the process of boating her. At that point two other members of the Oregon Inlet fleet contributed to help get the marlin on board: Charlie Griffin of the *Sea Witch* left his boat and came over to lend a hand, and the *Barbara B* loaned the crew an extra block and tackle.

"Seven guests and crew, and it still took us three hours to get her in," Piper said. Their efforts were rewarded by the number on the Pirate's Cove scales: 1,021 pounds. The fish hung on the scales all night guarded by Spina, who slept on the dock, and after it was mounted it went on display in the Pirate's Cove marina.

It's striking that every one of those four grander catches happened in the second half of August, proving what experienced Outer Banks captains have known for years about prime time for East Coast marlin. Late August, especially when the moon is full, brings famously fruitful marlin fishing outings.

Tales of successful grander hunts are certainly memorable, but blue marlin aren't the only sought-after fish with a starring role in dramatic Outer Banks fish stories in the latter part of the twentieth century. One such tale, a bluefin tuna adventure of epic proportions, drew countless anglers to Hatteras Inlet in 1995, also known as the year the blues came back. Bluefin tuna, which can grow as large as 2,000 pounds, were on every angler's bucket list back then, said Charles Perry, but sightings of the breed were few and far between. Old-timers remembered tales of a spate of bluefin in the 1950s, but by the mid-1990s most Outer Banks crew members had had few opportunities to catch a bluefin.

That all changed one day in March when Charles heard from Bull Tolson, a prolific commercial fisherman, that he had seen large quantities of bluefin tuna feeding on bluefish on a nearby wreck in 120 feet of water. Charles trusted that Tolson knew his stuff, and if his friend said he had seen bluefin in the area that was all Charles needed to plan a fishing trip. He and Paul Spencer left out of Oregon Inlet and ran down to Hatteras Inlet to fish in the area where the bluefin had been seen—a relatively shallow spot above a shipwreck site. It was more of an investigative trip than anything; they were using eighty-pound tackle which was, as it turned out, insufficient for what awaited them. On that first day they caught three or four in the 250-to-500-pound range, and they couldn't wait to go back the next day.

Perry and Spencer tied up their boat at the Hatteras Marlin Club, cleaned up from the day's fishing and got on the phone. Spencer called his regular charter customers, telling them to drop everything and get to Hatteras if at all possible. Charles called Peter Wright, his friend and a world-class fisherman, down in Florida, telling him, "We went out there and caught big bluefin, and we weren't even using the right kind of tackle." Wright told him to update him after he went out again and could prove that it was more than just one lucky day.

The next day the two men took out a charter on Spencer's boat with a setup better suited to the huge tuna, and they caught five. They still didn't have a harness, which they realized they needed to take full advantage of the situation, but it was an amazing fishing day nonetheless, and it proved to a growing number of observers that this bluefin bonanza was no fluke. When they got back to the marina, Perry hit the phone again. He called Wright and another friend, Gary Stuve, with whom he had fished for bluefin in the Bahamas, because he knew they loved bluefin fishing and might be willing to travel a long distance at the drop of a hat for such an opportunity.

Stuve and his friend Charlie Hayden drove all night to get there the next day, and on their first outing they caught fifteen bluefin. Every single day the haul got better, and a growing horde of fishermen docking their boats down there kept going out, wondering when their good fortune would hit its peak.

"When I fished for bluefin with Peter in the Bahamas, if we caught two or three a day it was a big day," Perry said. "It was really hard to catch them. I told Peter we had caught five, and he could hardly believe it." The next day, Perry had something even more unbelievable to report to his fishing friends worldwide. He and Spencer had gone out again, and on the third day they caught nine.

In his daily exultant phone call to Peter, he remembers that Wright was at a boat show in Miami, yelling, "CP caught nine bluefin up in Hatteras!" It was a scenario few anglers, even professionals, had ever encountered.

Eddie Smith, the owner of Grady-White Boats in Greenville and an avid fisherman himself, heard the scuttlebutt at the boat show too. When Wright asked him if he could quickly get some boats over to Hatteras, he finished his business and sent two Grady-White boats to the Outer Banks. Wright, Smith, and Perry went out for a couple of days and caught five or six more bluefin each day. It was a feeding frenzy; when anglers threw fatbacks (menhaden used as bait) into the water they would see the blues just bob up to the surface.

When Smith left with his boats, Wright got a boat up there from Florida, and the jackpot continued. Perry remembers one day with Wright on his boat the *Raptor* when they reeled in thirty-one bluefin. After one of those spectacular fishing days Perry also called Stewart Campbell, a legendary sportfisherman for whom Perry had worked as a wireman all over the world. "You can catch as many as you can crank in," Perry told Campbell.

It was Campbell who finally found that peak, on a day of fishing that none of his crewmates will ever forget. Wright, Stuve, Hayden, Perry, and John Rafter each played a role as Campbell reeled in dizzying seventy-three bluefin tuna in one day, all in the 300-to-500-pound class. "He sat in the chair for eleven-and-a-half hours, and we had thirteen sixty-pound cartons of fatbacks," Perry said. "It was amazing. And nobody will ever do it again for a couple of reasons. First, because physically I don't think anyone else could ever do it, and also because they'll never bite that good again in twenty fathoms of water."

Campbell died in 2010, but that day off the coast of the Southern Outer Banks will far outlive him. A 2018 *Marlin* magazine article recounting his manifold amazing fishing feats around the world led with the story of the seventy-three catches, calling it "the most epic day of giant bluefin tuna fishing ever recorded."

The most dramatic features on the Outer Banks fishing landscape of the 1980s and 1990s were these action-packed and historic catches offshore, but through those years there also ran an undercurrent of change related to technology and conservation that altered every aspect of life on the waterfront. The idea of releasing a big marlin, which was met with such incredulity when Jack and Elly Cleveland opted to do it from the *Albatross II* in 1958, slowly became accepted practice as the decade wore on.

Eventually the state and international fishing regulations would reflect this shift, but the organizers of local tournaments and the charter captains who drove fishing tourism moved toward more proactive release practices before they were required to by law. The premier tournament on Hatteras Island even changed its name to reflect the new policies – from the Hatteras Marlin Club International Blue Marlin Tournament to the Hatteras Marlin Club Blue Marlin Release Tournament. The Hatteras Marlin Club event is now release-only, while the Pirate's Cove Billfish Tournament allows only for the capture of blue marlin that exceed 110 inches or 400 pounds.

Another key development in the rise of conservation in North Carolina was the establishment of the North Carolina Governor's Cup in 1990. The Governor's Cup, which was renamed the North Carolina Billfish Series in 2021, is a series of eight billfish tournaments that operate each season on a cumulative point system, with a banquet celebrating the winning crew each fall. A key value of the series, which was managed until recently by the North Carolina Division of Marine Fisheries, is to promote conservation of the state's offshore fisheries.

Limits on captured fish during charter trips and lucrative release prizes in tournaments have significantly boosted conservation on the Outer Banks, and as the changes have become convention local captains and anglers have come to realize that more frequent catching and releasing doesn't diminish the excitement of a day when the bite is good in the Gulf Stream.

And it isn't just more stringent regulations that have led to more robust conservation of the fish species off the Outer Banks; more humane tackle like circle hooks and intensified research and tagging initiatives have fortified coastal conservation efforts as well.

One of the longest running tagging programs, "Tag-A-Giant," has its roots in that Hatteras bluefin tuna bonanza in the 1990s. Since its formation in 1994, Tag-A-Giant has caught more than 2,000 bluefin and equipped them with sophisticated devices that allow scientists to collect detailed data about their migratory patterns, body temperature, and other physiological details. It's a program that has given a wealth of information to marine biologists eager to protect the beautiful and coveted fish, and it all came about because a group of stalwart anglers crossed paths with a much larger group of bluefin one winter and spread the word. It's one more key piece of the Outer Banks' enduring fishing legacy, which adds dramatic chapters even through seasons of change.

Outer Banks Boat Builders at 2022 tournament, with all proceeds going towards scholarships for children from families associated with boat building. Sitting from left to right: Bobby Croswait, Ernie Foster, Paul Spencer, Sunny Briggs, Billy Maxwell. Standing left to right: Daniel Spencer, Aaron Croswait, Jordie Croswait, Paul Mann, Patrick Harrison, John R. Bayliss, John Bayliss, Valentin Manuel, Ricky Scarborough Jr., Jeffrey Blackwell, Bo Meekins, Kurt Daniels, Ritchie Howell

CHAPTER 9

Elevating the Standards

Located on the southern tip of Roanoke Island on the Outer Banks, Wanchese has fewer than 2,000 residents and no discernible downtown, but it is the home to many of the busiest and most prestigious boatbuilding companies anywhere in the world.

A quick tour of this custom boat creation hotbed might start at Spencer Yachts, where Paul Spencer has built 120 hulls over the past twenty-five years, before heading across the island to see the showpieces coming out of Bayliss Boatworks and the custom builds from Blackwell Boatworks with a final stop at the birthplace of the classic Carolina sportfishing vessels of Scarborough Boatworks. In previous decades, pioneers like Omie Tillett, Sunny Briggs, Billy Holton, and Ricky Scarborough, whose son now runs the company he founded, have also constructed their boats in Wanchese.

Each of the current companies has its own distinct twist, but Paul Spencer, John Bayliss, Craig Blackwell, and Ricky Scarborough all have their roots in the storied boatbuilding heritage of the Outer Banks. They have all spent untold hours fishing offshore themselves, both because they love being out on the water and because they know it's impossible to build an excellent sportfishing boat without a lived-in understanding of the conditions that boat will be asked to thrive in.

In all the ways that matter, those modern boatbuilders, and their contemporaries further south in Hatteras and in other pockets along the North Carolina coast, are cut from the same cloth as Warren O'Neal, Buddy Cannady, Buddy Davis, and Omie Tillett. Like those early mentors they place a high premium on hard work, dependable designs, and the unique spirit of the community in which they fish, build, live and play. But the successful builders of today are also characterized by the myriad ways in which they have diverged from the early pioneers, differences spurred by the frantic pace of technology and the effect of that galloping progress on the world of sportfishing.

Warren O'Neal died more than twenty years ago, but if he could somehow visit a shop like Bayliss Boatworks today he would surely be astounded by the cutting-edge advancements being applied to every stage of the construction process. Bayliss's painting building, with top-of-the-line filtration and machines designed to keep every particle of dust out, is the first of its kind for sportfishing boats, and it gives boats perfect, smooth paint coverage with just one coat. Six of Bayliss's employees do nothing but draft designs for boat parts on a computer, and when they have perfected each component on the screen they use a 3-D printer to create a scale model of the part to make sure it will work perfectly on the boat-in-progress.

In spring 2023, the crews at both Bayliss and Spencer were working on several boats that were eighty feet or longer—a size that would have completely astounded the captains promoting the area's first charter businesses in the 1950s and 1960s. Spencer is tinkering with a jet-powered boat that can move faster and more efficiently out to the Gulf Stream but still troll smoothly at slower speeds when anglers put out their spreads.

In the same way that captains all over the world will specifically request an Oregon Inlet mate if they want a crew member who has fished in all types of conditions, Carolina sportfishing vessels are praised and sought after in every busy fishing port around the globe. One highly regarded boatbuilder, Merritt's in Florida, sends would-be clients up the coast when they come in looking for a sportfishing boat, said Spencer. He tells them, "If you want a yacht, come here. If you're looking for a sportfishing boat, go to Oregon Inlet."

Boatbuilding ventures like these have struck a dynamic balance between honoring the craft's heritage and keeping pace with new techniques, materials, and components that can help boats perform better. Their place in the story is solidly on the bridge between past and future, as they seek to uphold the legacy that enabled their own chapter while still embracing the unceasing pattern of progress that governs the industry now.

Paul Spencer grew up in Manns Harbor, a small Outer Banks village on the mainland side of the bridge across from Roanoke Island. Manns Harbor is a third of the size of Wanchese but is nonetheless the birthplace of several prominent anglers and boatbuilders, including Spencer and original Dykstra's captains Chick Craddock and Clarence Holmes. Spencer's older brother Duke had been a mate for Tillett, and Spencer couldn't imagine a more exciting life than that, he said. So when he was thirteen he ventured over the bridge to Oregon Inlet and took a job as a mate for Craddock. Before too long, he also got a turn at his dream job mating for Tillett on board the *Sportsman*.

After a few years of working as a mate, Spencer met Shelly Midgett, the daughter of Oregon Inlet captain and boatbuilder Sheldon Midgett. The two started dating, which led Spencer to an offseason job in Midgett's boat shop, making two dollars an hour to do, as he said, "the jobs that nobody else wanted." He sanded, painted, mixed the epoxy glue and learned how to lay out the juniper planks for a boat's hull. He was usually drafted to paint in the smallest, most cramped parts of the boat, in the days before it occurred to anyone to wear a respirator or even a paper mask.

"I had to crawl down in the bilge and paint it out, with this old lead-based paint that was terrible," he said. "Nobody knew what a respirator was back then, either. I remember crawling down in the bilge of a boat to paint, and when I crawled out I couldn't stand up for a while; all I could do was just crawl."

Paul and Shelly married when they were still teenagers, and he continued the common Outer Banks rhythm of working on a crew during the fishing months and assisting his father-in-law with his boats during the offseason. Midgett had a 100-foot building, an unusually large shop for the time, in which he typically built two boats simultaneously. Spencer remembers the amazement in the Oregon Inlet community when he built a fifty-foot vessel he named the *Fishing Fool II*. No one in that area had seen a boat that size before, and the only place they could find to launch it was a cement boat ramp at the Manteo Airport.

After building close to twenty hulls, Midgett decided to retire from boatbuilding and return to his charter business full-time, but not before he topped his previous accomplishment and built a fifty-five-footer for himself. By that time Spencer had spent many of his offseasons helping with his own father's commercial fishing operation, and he had also become a captain and started running boats for other owners. After Midgett ran the *Fishing Fool II* for a while he sold it to his son-in-law, who renamed it the *Sizzler*. Spencer couldn't get over the boat's size. "I remember getting it and thinking, 'It's so big, I think you could land a helicopter on the bow deck,'" he said.

Spencer and his wife had five children, and the long, irregular hours of commercial fishing were keeping him away from home far too much. After one such long night he told his wife, "We've got to do something different." He had been inside enough boatbuilding shops to believe he could try his hand at it, and he was particularly intrigued by the practice of Buddy Cannady, who built one boat every winter, fished with it through the season, and then sold it. He always had a new boat to use for his charter business, and then he could make a profit each fall.

Once he committed to his new course, Spencer was all in. He knew that if he was going to have enough funds to build a boat, he would need to sell the *Sizzler*. He and Shelly decided that the wise thing to do was to take the proceeds and pay off their house, so that if boatbuilding was a bust they would still have a roof over their heads. After they did that, Spencer applied for several loans to build his first shop and buy the supplies he needed, and the seedling of Spencer Yachts was planted.

His first area of focus was the design of the boat. Spencer knew about the evolution of the Carolina sportfishing hulls that had made vessels sleeker and faster, but he wasn't satisfied with just a copy of someone else's design. He wanted to incorporate the look of the Florida boats he liked the best with the "Carolina flare" the area had become known for. Then a conversation with Billy Baum gave him a non-negotiable for the bottom of the boat. "Billy came to me and said, 'You've got to put this delta conic bottom on it,'" Spencer said. "He sat down and explained it to me, and I said, 'OK.' When we first ran the boat we were just so impressed with it. We thought it ran better than anything else around. I said, 'Man, we can change anything on this boat but the bottom.'"

At first, as planned, Spencer turned out one boat a year, but a triumph he had on board his second boat, the *Anticipation*, accelerated his timeline considerably. The owner of the *Anticipation* asked him to be the captain in 1999 when they took the boat to the White Marlin Open in Ocean City, Maryland, one of the largest billfish tournaments in the nation. Spencer's boat won first and second place, and his share of the winnings—$160,000—allowed him to build a second boat shop in Manns Harbor and upgrade his first, which was just a tin shed with no electricity, no doors, and no plumbing. There's no shot in the arm to a boatbuilder like one of his hulls passing the fleet in a tournament and bringing back one of the largest fish. Suddenly he was fielding frequent phone calls from anglers asking, "Can I have one of those?"

A year later Spencer won the White Marlin Open again, enabling him to build a third boat shop. He was turning out three boats a year at that point, but the demand soon outpaced the space he had in Manns Harbor, and he started looking for land. With the help of a friend, he was able to buy the old Sportsman's Boatworks facility in Wanchese, which had originally belonged to Omie Tillett. Like that fifty-five-footer years earlier, the five-acre property seemed intimidatingly large to Spencer at first, but it didn't take long for him to expand his operations to fit the space.

Where some businesspeople are risk-averse, Spencer is the exact opposite. He embraces the risk associated with new ideas, even when they don't work initially. It has never bothered him to be the first boatbuilder in the area to try a bigger engine, a different cabin shape, or new technology and building techniques. His philosophy can be summed up simply: "It's just a boat; it's just wood and glue. If I don't like it, I'll change it."

Spencer is so willing to dive into untested waters that sometimes he finds himself in over his head, and he has to task his team with solving the problems that their new models have created. A prime example was the burst in speed they experienced, soon after they moved into the Wanchese facility in the early 2000s, when Caterpillar offered him the prototype of a new and powerful engine. Suddenly Spencer's client had a boat that could run forty-four knots and cruise at forty, which was speed no one in Oregon Inlet had encountered before. The faster vessel brought complications like wheel burn and rudder blowout, but as Spencer sees it the process of tweaking to fix those issues is just the cost of staying on the cutting edge.

"Any time you cover new ground there are some challenges and there's a learning curve, but that's the way you get ahead," he said.

"People in the sportfishing world don't accept change very well. If you step way out of the box, you'll get a bunch of negativity. You have to do it and prove it. But if something doesn't work at first I take that as a challenge, not a brick wall."

In 2023 Spencer's team was simultaneously working on seven boats over seventy feet long, which would have completely flummoxed Paul and his fellow young mates who could hardly come to grips with a fifty-foot boat in the previous century. He has had to cut openings in some of his shops, which weren't built to accommodate boats of that size. And the innovations just keep coming. Recently he had a client ask if the bow of his boat could open at the touch of a button, like in a James Bond movie, to reveal the anchor. A Spencer engineer, Hal Simmons, figured out a way to make it happen.

John Bayliss found his way into boatbuilding accidentally when he was faced with a career crossroads in the wake of the September 11 attacks. A native of California, Bayliss's family moved frequently in his youth. He grew up bottom fishing with his father on the west coast, but the most consequential decision his dad made was the summer he packed up the family for a vacation at Hatteras. Bayliss was so taken with the Outer Banks, and especially the variety and richness of the fishing there, that he made it his goal to get back and work in those waters as soon as he could. "I remember distinctly, I think I was twelve, and we were riding home—you know, family station wagon, had a great trip, all that jazz—and I was telling myself, 'I've got to find a way to go do this' " he said.

Not too many years later, Bayliss called Emory Dillon, the legendary Hatteras captain who had taken the Bayliss family fishing on that trip. He asked Dillon if he needed a mate, and before long Dillon called him back to tell him he had an opening. Bayliss got himself to the Outer Banks as quickly as he could. That was 1975, and even as his role in the fishing industry has evolved over almost fifty years, his love of the area and the excitement of being out on the water has never waned.

After five years as a mate, Bayliss started running his own boat and fishing commercially in the offseason. He sold his charter boat in 1997 and took a job running the company sportfishing boat for Hatteras Yachts, which is based in New Bern, North Carolina. He didn't know it at the time, but that position with a large boatbuilding company actually paved the way for what would become his life's work. "I was going to boat shows, talking to customers," he said. "I was getting spoon fed all of this information, having zero desire, zero idea we were going to be building boats."

From Hatteras Yachts he took a job running a private boat, but that opportunity ended abruptly after September 11, 2001. He seriously considered buying a commercial boat and going back to longlining, but before committing to that course he decided to put out a couple of feelers to see if anyone wanted him to build them a boat. Before he even had a shop four people had placed orders for boats, so he bought a building and started his first hull on April 15, 2002.

It's been an eventful two decades for Bayliss Boatworks: twenty-seven completed hulls, a community of loyal customers who come back to Bayliss for second, third, and fourth boats, and the ongoing expansion of their sprawling headquarters in Wanchese. Bayliss and his team are known for their meticulous attention to detail, for holding every detail of every boat to a high standard. The resulting crafts are true luxury sportfishing boats, like *Reel Wheels II,* Bayliss's largest build as of 2023. The 90-footer, originally named *Singularis,* features five staterooms, six heads, and teak and marble accents throughout the cabin.

Every detail of each boat is customized, originating from thorough conversations with the customer followed by transparent timelines and budgets to ensure that those future Bayliss boat owners encounter no surprises along the way. If they come to Bayliss, they know they're committing to a boatbuilding process that could take up to two years with hundreds of dedicated labor hours committed to a single vessel.

"While there are plenty of incredible skills involved throughout the boat building process, watching a wooden hull being carefully sculpted like they do at Bayliss may be the most captivating," reads an article about Bayliss on PeterMillar.com. "From the raw sheets of Okoume wood sourced from Africa, to the patient hand-sanding, to the thousands upon thousands of golf tees used to fill in screw holes after the wood is set in place, the comprehensive detail required on such a behemoth scale is staggering."

As surprised as he would have been about the fact a quarter-century ago, Bayliss has found his true calling in the bustling, sprawling operation that is Bayliss Boatworks. He still loves to fish and compete in tournaments, but he has learned that boatbuilding allows for predictable outcomes in a way that a fishing day offshore never can. "The fishing thing, you do all your study, all your research, and you think, 'I've got all this figured out,' " he said. "You don't have anything figured out. This is more exacting. If you put in the time and work hard at it, you can put something in the water and say, 'That's exactly what I thought it was going to look like.' "

Spencer, Bayliss, and Blackwell, who worked with Buddy Davis before starting his own operation in 1988, each started their careers on charter boats and stumbled into boatbuilding, but the other major boatbuilder in Wanchese, Ricky Scarborough Jr., was literally born into the career path. Scarborough's father Ricky Scarborough Sr. built his first boat in 1977, and a year later he built a shop on the same property where his son operates Scarborough Boatworks today. As the state's longest operating boat company, Scarborough has forged a reputation for sleek, effective fishing crafts. When a local was once asked to describe the quintessential Carolina fishing boat, he responded by saying, "That's a Ricky boat."

More than any other Outer Banks boatbuilder working today, Scarborough has lived through the changes in construction techniques and technological developments. He worked alongside his father for twenty years before taking over the company in 2010, and he still remembers the day he realized that under his leadership they could no longer construct each hull using the old plank-on-frame method.

Building with plank-on-frame meant that Scarborough had to be present for every step of the fairing and planking processes, while still keeping up with the business aspects of the company. One day he was about to leave for Pensacola, Florida to measure for a customer's mezzanine, he said, but a build-in-process needed his constant attention. "I'm on the stage, with a cellphone in one pocket, the shop phone clipped to the other one, a grinder in my hand and a mask on," he recounted in a 2019 episode of the "Boat Builders Reel Talk" podcast. "And every time I would have to stop to take off that mask and put the grinder down, to answer the phone, the five guys working with me had to stop, too. I got on the plane, my brother was with me, and I said, 'I will not do this for the next twenty years of my life.' It was a pretty easy decision from that point on."

Any observer at a big marina or a popular billfish tournament, where an Omie Tillett craft from the 1960s might be anchored offshore alongside a Wanchese-built boat from 2020, can observe the dramatic changes in boatbuilding over the years, and Scarborough said that he is grateful for anything that makes boats safer and more comfortable. Even though technology like seakeepers and sonar are key elements to that growth, he said that increasing access to more powerful engines has been the primary driver for hulls that have doubled in average size since charter fishing took off in the 1950s.

"Nobody downsizes," he said on the podcast. "Man is always trying to do something faster, bigger, better than the last one they did, and I think more horsepower has been the catalyst for that." With a customer base that seems to lean toward young families, Scarborough said that he is gratified that he and his crew have cemented his father's legacy while remaining nimble enough to keep pace with those changes.

"I am very proud that my father and I have been in business for forty years," he said. "Not many boatbuilders can say that. A lot of boatbuilders have come and gone in that time span. And hopefully we haven't just endured but we have continued to grow. When our boats are no longer relevant, no longer catch people's eye, then it's time to quit."

New boatbuilders hang out their shingle regularly on the Outer Banks, but the keepers of the area's fishing history share Scarborough's gratitude that the craftsmen who started building the legendary Carolina sportfishing boats a half century ago produced descendants like Scarborough, Spencer, and Bayliss. Those men, keepers of the flame, have remained faithful to principles like creativity, innovation, and community while still taking enough risks to compete in the bigger, faster, more powerful market that dominates the sportfishing world today.

Kenny Jo with a sword he carved from a swordfish bill, complete with macramé handle

Kenny Jo: A True Original

Kenny Johansen didn't own a car or a home, and he was only concerned with money inasmuch as a pay day aboard a charter boat could buy him a meal and some beers at his favorite watering hole. He had served time in his early years, so after a period behind bars he spent the rest of his life pursuing the freest existence he could imagine: serving as a mate on boats from the Florida Keys to the Outer Banks.

Kenny Jo, as he was known to all, was a beloved and unique character who spent every fishing season at Oregon Inlet, signing on as a mate with any captain who appreciated his kindness and experience. When the weather got cooler and the fish moved on, he would either hitchhike or ride a bus down to Florida, where he had more captain friends ready to sign him onto their crews. As his friend Charles Perry wrote in a tribute after Kenny Jo's death, "There was never a time in his life when he could not put all his possessions in one bag and immediately head off to a new destination."

When Kenny Jo died in 2020, his friends donated money to make sure that his clear wish, to be cremated and scattered over the waters of the Atlantic off the Outer Banks, could be fulfilled. Everyone who knew the itinerant mate agrees on a couple of things: he lived life on his terms, he never said no to a drink, and he was the subject of enough stories to fill a substantial book. Just a sampling of those tales is sufficient to explain why everyone who remembers Kenny Jo quickly gets around to describing him in the same way: one of a kind.

- Kenny Jo liked to stay out late drinking at a favorite spot like RV's in Kitty Hawk, but he also knew that he wouldn't get hired as a mate if he couldn't make the before-dawn call time at the docks. On one particular night he was afraid he wouldn't get up in time after a big night out, so he got a friend to drive him to the Oregon Inlet Fishing Center, found the boat he was set to work on the next day, crawled into the fish box and fell fast asleep. A few hours later the captain and the charter party arrived, and they saw no sign of Kenny Jo. The captain said, "Look, I'm supposed to have a mate here but he hasn't showed up yet, so we just need to leave without him." They had just run out a mile or two when Kenny Jo emerged bleary-eyed from the fish box, ready to work.

- Everyone who spent much time around him considered Kenny Jo a friend, and he was always quick to help his friends with anything they needed, but he also loved a good practical joke. One of his most legendary pranks involved a potted meat sandwich, and its target was friend and fellow mate Wayne Johnson, better known around the fishing center as "Snooky." On one fishing trip Kenny Jo made potted meat sandwiches for the crew, but instead of meat he put dog food inside Snooky's sandwich. When Snooky took a bite, he commented that it didn't taste much like potted meat, but he ate it anyway, hungry from a day on the water. For months afterward, Kenny Jo barked every time he saw Snooky.

- When he wasn't fishing in warmer climates during the offseason, Kenny Jo would find work as a house painter, but money was only useful to him in helping him drink and pay rent for the modest rooms he would occupy on his various stops. One day he had a paycheck from a painting job and he got a ride with two other members of the painting crew to the bank to cash his check. He asked the teller for his money in ones and fives, and his companions asked, "Kenny Jo, do you have a poker game coming up?" When they pulled away from the bank and started down the bypass, Kenny Jo crumpled up one of the one-dollar bills, rolled the window down and tossed it out, then did it again with more of the ones, then the fives. His friends said, "Kenny Jo, what in the world are you doing?" He answered, "I can see that none of you boys have ever done any hitchhiking. I'm going to make someone's day."

- One day Kenny Jo, while longlining offshore with Perry, was battling a shark he had on the leader. He got his arm caught on a raised nail on a baiting table and cut a deep six-to-eight-inch gash on his forearm. He wrapped it up in what Perry described as a whole roll of paper towels and lots of duct tape, until Perry finally convinced him to unwrap it so he could check out the wound. When he saw the cut Perry knew he had to sew it up himself, because it would take so long for them to get to shore and see a doctor. He had proper sutures, but only rusty fishing pliers as a surgical tool, and Kenny Jo directed him through every stitch, perfectly calm with no indication that he felt any pain throughout the stitching. (He did, however, finish all but one of the beers in the six-pack Perry had brought on the trip.)

• Although it happened in the Florida Keys, one of the most memorable Kenny Jo stories also involved a serious arm wound, this one sustained when a friend pulled his truck near Kenny Jo's bicycle on the side of the road and accidentally caught him with the big A-frame side mirror. He resisted going to the hospital in Miami until he almost lost the arm to gangrene; his arm was only saved after an intense regimen of antibiotics and ten days in the hospital. When he was about to be released, he had been in conversations with the insurance company representing the man who was driving the truck, and he wrote a letter stipulating that he wanted $10,000 in cash in exchange for keeping the issue out of court. He got his money, went back to the Keys, and gave $1,000 to the bartender at his favorite spot so all of his friends could drink. He kept replenishing the tab and also bought plenty of pot for himself and his buddies, until it was time to go back to North Carolina. After ten days of partying and a bus trip north, he had $20 and an ounce of pot left.

• Kenny Jo was easy to get along with unless you lived with him and made a mess of the place, as his friend Mike Bennett learned one day in Kitty Hawk. Kenny Jo had just washed the dishes, cleaned the kitchen until it shined, and gone out to RVs, when Bennett and his girlfriend ate a meal and left their dirty dishes in the sink. They weren't there when Kenny Jo returned, and he promptly took the dirty dishes out of the sink, along with all the clean dishes in the cabinet, and threw them into the trash bag. Then he went into Bennett's room, found his credit card and ordered a new set of dishes. When Bennett returned, incredulous, and found a trash can full of broken dishes, Kenny Jo told him, "If you can't keep 'em clean there's no use in having 'em."

Kenny Jo was a mate to all in more than one sense of the word, and his carefree lifestyle fit perfectly with the vibe of the Outer Banks marinas, waterways, and bars he loved.

Charter Boat Captains, Oregon Inlet Fishing Center, Shrine Club, Wanchese, NC, circa 1955. Front row (left to right): Willie Etheridge Jr., *Chi Chi*; Billy Baum, *Kay*; Harry Baum, *Jo-Boy*; Marvin Daniels, *Mar-Pete*; Moon Tillett, *Bumbaloo*; Fred Basnight, *Slow and Easy*; Charles Midgett, *Lois C*; Leee Dough, *Libby D*; Warren O'Neal, *Pearl*; Melvin Perry, *Golden Dawn*; Wayland Baum, *Alethia*. Back row (left to right): Tony Tillett, *Carolinian*; Omie Tillett, *Sportsman*; Buddy Cannady, *Mel-O-Dee*; H.T. Gaskins, *Erma Queen*; Carson Stallings, *Carrov*; Warren Gallop, *Margie C*; Kenneth Ward, *Cherokee*; Jesse Etheridge, *Caredwyn*; Lee Perry, *Deepwater*

CHAPTER 10

A Lasting Legacy

The sportfishing arms race that brings ever longer, faster, and more technologically equipped boats to the Outer Banks would also seem to multiply the size and quantity of the fish captured in those waters, but old-timers know that the latest and greatest doesn't always bring in the prize catch. Bobby Scarborough is the very definition of an Outer Banks lifer—a native of Hatteras whose grandfather built some of the earliest sportfishing boats in the area and who has fished on charters in both Oregon Inlet and Hatteras over the past sixty years—and he often sees new custom boats with major horsepower and fuel capacity run fast and far offshore, unaware of how many fish they're driving over on their high-speed journey.

Scarborough and Charles Perry have a ready supply of stories of triumphant fishing accomplishments that occurred just a few miles offshore, like the time in the 1950s when Capt. Joe Berry caught a big marlin just four miles from the coast, or Omie Tillett's tale about the day he caught several sailfish within sight of the sea buoy. When Perry was a young mate with Capt. Murray Cudworth, he recalls a particularly productive day on the *Mar-T-Moe*, a boat that maxed out at just fourteen knots.

"It was one of the slowest boats out there," Perry said. "We were doing fourteen knots and that was as fast as we could go. But we caught twenty-five blue marlin in one season, and fourteen of those were caught coming and going." In other words, when headed offshore for a day of sportfishing, the journey often holds just as many treasures as the destination—if you slow down enough to look.

Sailfish, in particular, tend to congregate far closer to the shoreline than most anglers expect, Scarborough said. He remembers one fall king mackerel trip when his party caught seven sails on the way out to their mackerel spot, and just in the past few years both he and Perry have heard tales of nice sailfish hookups in just twenty fathoms of water.

Look for prize fish on the way out to the Gulf Stream. Don't be in such a hurry that you miss the riches swimming right under your boat as you motor by. It's the kind of wisdom that the older captains in the area have in spades, the gems that are readily available to the new generation of anglers if they only stop to have a cup of coffee and listen. The twenty-first century along the Outer Banks has been marked by an underlying tension between hard-won insight of the waters and the modern advantages represented by sensitive sonar systems and eighty-foot boats. The key, for anyone wanting to get the very most out of a Hatteras or Oregon Inlet fishing expedition, is to figure out how to mine the gems of both the storied past and the cutting-edge future.

In the first decade of the new century, two major blue marlin catches in a three-year period out of Oregon Inlet reminded charter clients and captains alike that the Outer Banks is still one of the most exciting fishing spots on the planet. The first, on a sunny day in late June of 2005, came on Capt. Arch Bracher's boat the *Pelican*.

The story of how Bracher and angler Jesse Waltz reeled in a 915-pound, 130-inch marlin is the kind of fish tale that crew members can recount for the rest of their lives and never fail to find rapt listeners. After a few tuna and dolphin catches, Bracher looked down that morning and saw a huge fish chasing a thirty-pound yellowfin tuna. Before the crew could even make a plan, the tuna and its massive pursuer went under the boat and out of sight. Bracher liked to keep a pitching rig on his boat for just such a situation; he would hook the smaller fish quickly, put it on the pitching rig and throw it back in front of the marlin in hopes he would grab it. But he didn't have the rig ready, so as fast as he could he scurried down the ladder and connected 80-pound line on a heavy rod.

After a bit of effort they hooked the tuna and got it onto the pitching rig, and soon the marlin was attached to the rig. But something was off; they could still see the tuna, and soon they realized the marlin was foul-hooked, the term for a fish that is hooked anywhere other than its mouth. Foul-hooked fish are notoriously hard to bring in, so Waltz was in for an epic tussle as the marlin was also tangled in the leader. After an intense wrestling match for ninety minutes, when the marlin was just feet from the boat, it died. It took six people to pull the huge fish through the transom door. "The odds of catching a fish like that, the way we did, and getting him in, it's like the lottery," Bracher told *The Washington Post* in an article detailing the catch.

By the time Bracher backed the *Pelican* into the weigh station at the Oregon Inlet Fishing Center a huge crowd had gathered, determined to catch a glimpse of the biggest marlin some had ever seen. At 915 pounds, it was the largest fish boated off the Outer Banks since the 1,085-pounder brought in by the *Teaser* thirteen years earlier. But it wouldn't be long before an even heavier marlin would gather an even larger crowd, because it was caught during tournament competition.

It was the morning of August 12, 2008—the final day of the Pirate's Cove Billfish Tournament. Capt. Mike King and his crew on the *Mimi* had a bite on a big artificial lure called Blue Breakfast. Angler Trey Irvine strapped into the fighting chair and began a tug of war that lasted more than two hours. Like other crews that have been the cast of characters in historic catches they suspected, even hoped, that they were dealing with an unusually large marlin. But just catching the first glimpse of the fish was only the first step in an unforgettable episode of man-versus-beast.

Paul Spencer, who built the *Mimi*, and his son Cliff were both part of the crew that day. The Pirate's Cove event awards points both for released billfish and for boated fish over 400 pounds, and Capt. King knew that his boat didn't have enough releases for the week to be in contention for the trophy. The alternative was to chase one big fish, so they set their coordinates to a good spot they knew northeast of Oregon Inlet and commenced the hunt.

About an hour after they lowered their spread into the glassy water, Spencer heard King yell "Short rigger!" The surface of the water was unusually calm, so when Spencer got his first glimpse of the marlin he already estimated it at 800 pounds or larger. Trey Irvine, the owner of *Mimi*, took control of the rod and worked the line as the massive fish tail walked, jumped and swam away. A man can't overpower a fish of that size; in situations like that the key is outmaneuvering it with proper angling and boat handling techniques and plenty of patience.

With years of experience boating big blues, Spencer coached the crew, especially in those crucial moments when the marlin, which looked to Spencer like a submarine, was subdued enough for them to hold close to the boat. As mate Patrick Byrd grabbed the leader, Cliff Spencer and Chris Hall Jr. hit the fish with three quick, strategically placed gaff shots. "We knew then it was a 'Holy Cow, it was something special down there,'" first mate Patrick Byrd told the *Wilmington Star-News*.

With all eight men laboring for some forty minutes to get the fish up on the deck, they had to pull it around the chair and lay its bill on the mezzanine because it was far too big to fit in the fifty-nine-foot vessel. That configuration made it nearly impossible to get an accurate measurement as to the fish's length, but they measured a tail-stump girth of twenty-one inches, and they knew that a stump over twenty inches usually corresponds to a marlin over 1,000 pounds. They radioed back to Pirate's Cove that they were en route with a truly dramatic fourth-quarter finish to the tournament, caught their breath, and enjoyed the ride back towards Outer Banks fame.

When the catch was eventually certified by the IGFA, it became the largest blue marlin ever caught off the coast of North Carolina, a record that still stood fifteen years later. The fish, which in addition to weighing 1,228 pounds and eight ounces measured at nearly 180 inches long, was also the third-largest marlin ever caught in the Atlantic Ocean, after a second-place catch in Cape Verde and the top marlin, a 1,402-pounder caught off the coast of Brazil in 1992. The *Mimi's* trophy fell to fourth place in the standings in 2022, when a marlin brought in at Cape Verde weighed in at 1,370 pounds.

The crew of the *Mimi* won the tournament that year, as the rules stipulate that a boat collects two points per pound of a captured marlin if the fish weighs over 400 pounds. That gave Irvine, King, and the others almost 2,500 points—a significant edge over the previous leaders who had been collecting 100 points per billfish they released.

Not everyone in the sportfishing world has a big marlin story like the ones associated with the *Pelican* and the *Mimi,* but Charles Perry is quick to emphasize that blue marlin only represent one plotline in a complex and exciting story. Since Perry is intimately acquainted with Cape Verde and every other major fishing hot spot in the world, he knows that the measure of a truly exceptional fishing destination is less about size and more about quantity and variety.

Some charter customers come to the Outer Banks chasing that once-in-a-lifetime moment with an enormous marlin, but for many others the calculus has more to do with the value of the fish they can take home to stock their freezers. Dolphin, wahoo, yellowfin

BIG FISH BETTER BOATS

tuna, amberjack, just to name a few, are known to be some of the tastiest fish out there, so groups will pony up several thousand dollars for an offshore trip with the hope that they can haul in fish whose worth equals or surpasses what they spent on the outing.

"We've had meat fisherman come down and back in with their coolers and all they want to do is fill them," Perry said. "The dolphin, wahoo, yellowfin tuna are the stabilizing force, especially the tuna. The limit for dolphin is sixty and for yellowfin is eighteen, and it's not unusual for a group to catch the limit and then go out to catch something else."

In a sense, Kenneth Brown symbolizes the complete history of the Outer Banks' evolution from little-known island chain to major sportfishing destination. His grandfather was the prolific Dare County publicity director Aycock Brown, whose creative commitment to spreading the word about the size and scope of fish that were coming in from Oregon and Hatteras inlets did more than anything else to ignite a tourism industry in an area that was, prior to World War II, all but unreachable from much of the East Coast.

Brown started mating for his father Billy at age eight, and through his college years at North Carolina State University he worked as Omie Tillett's mate on board the *Sportsman*. As he tells it, he moved to Virginia after graduating with an engineering degree and worked "a real job" just long enough to convince his girlfriend Liz to become his wife, but the call of the sea was too deafening to ignore. He returned to the Outer Banks as a mate, working first for Brynner Parks on the *Smoker* and then for Tony Tillett on the *Carolinian,* before finally taking the helm of his own boat, the *Trophy Hunter.*

Brown embraces many aspects of progress in the sportfishing world, using new technology as he fishes out of Oregon Inlet on his boat, but he believes seasoned and young anglers alike should take a measured approach to the rapid change along the waterfront, so that the valued elements forged in the past don't get obscured. "Instead of fighting the growth, we should mold the growth so that it works for the future," he said. "In my granddad's day it was like a frontier down here. Any kind of growth was moving forward. But nowadays you have to be more careful about growth."

Once an eager teenager hoping to learn from legends like the Tilletts and the Fosters, Brown is now one of the veterans of the waterfront, competing every day with younger captains who have the latest and greatest tech aboard their vessels. He and others of his generation, men like Bull Tolson and Buddy Hooper, continue to be amazed at the volume of fish brought into the docks, despite the sustained tourist boom multiplying the number of boats competing for the catches. Tolson, who started working as a captain in 1984, was part of an extraordinary 2022 yellowfin tuna bonanza. During one thirty-day period, he said, there were at least 150 boats fishing out of Oregon Inlet and each one was bringing in fifteen to twenty yellowfin every day. A member of the fishing center staff told him that in one single day that May, they cleaned 50,000 pounds of tuna.

Tolson notes that the water temperatures are warmer and the various fishing seasons have shifted accordingly, but from the bluefin arrivals early in the calendar year to the yellowfins in the spring and big marlin in late summer and early fall, the opportunities for historic fishing days continue unabated along North Carolina's barrier islands. The thrill is still there for fishermen of all ages, but the veterans can't help but wonder if their younger counterparts are starting to lose some of the elements that have set this fishing area apart.

When Brown suggests that charter captains don't have to embrace progress at any cost, he's concerned that the younger generation might miss the thrill of the hunt, the creativity required when one fishery is fruitless and you have to adapt your spread and search for the right location to make it a good day. Technology can be fantastic, but none of the men who took the baton from the pioneers in Hatteras or Oregon Inlet want offshore fishing to become an automated, predictable experience. The magic is found when a crew knows the waters and works hard, but still goes out every day expecting surprises.

Fish-finding capabilities and boats that reach the Gulf Stream at record speed aren't the only changes with the potential to alter the area's unique identity as a fishing destination. The most vital intangible out on these waters, the core value that has made the area special, is the cooperation and camaraderie among the anglers. Brown, Tolson, and Hooper can't count the number of times they have seen a boat come into the slip with a mechanical issue and every captain and mate within shouting distance offers to help diagnose and fix the problem.

It's a fishing culture forged by men who learned to drive big boats when they were too young to reach the steering wheel, but their daddies had trained them so well that they sent them out anyway with a box for a step stool. It's an environment where men gathered until the late hours at Sam and Omie's drinking beer and swapping stories, and they could be trusted to lock up after the owner went to bed. It's a place where relationships among crew members are so valued that when Capt. Emory Dillon of Hatteras died in 2013, he requested that three specific men spread his ashes out over the deep—his former mates John Bayliss, Buddy Hooper, and Chip Shafer.

Before he started a fifty-plus-year career that took him to fishing spots from Costa Rica to Baja, California, Shafer cut his teeth on charter boats in Hatteras and Oregon inlets, and he learned quickly that success wasn't predicated merely on the number of fish a captain brought in each day. They might have used friendly competitiveness in hopes of besting their dockmates, he said, but keeping quiet about prime fishing spots was discouraged. At the end of the day, the fleet was in it together, he said, and he has carried that spirit of unity with him ever since.

"If you were the guy that could put the fleet on some fish, you were the hero that far transcended what you could catch yourself that day," he said. "Better to put the guys on fish than to catch a bunch yourself. You wouldn't last there long if you came in with a load of fish, never said a word about it, and nobody else had done very well. That wouldn't play well at all."

Perry and Shafer have been able to see the world from the decks of fishing boats, but even though they have enjoyed the variety of scenery and people throughout their journeys, they have always known that their first fishing home can compete in every way with the more high-profile or exotic destinations where they found themselves. Perry, whose father and two uncles were three of the original Dykstra's Ditch trailblazers, said that he has enormous respect for many of the captains and mates he encounters around Oregon Inlet and Hatteras. He and Shafer cut their teeth on the Outer Banks, so they know better than most that the volume, variety, and challenge of fishing there, as well as the exceptional camaraderie between the men who rise early each day to rig their baits, is second-to-none.

"I'm extremely proud of the men that I have fished around and the names that we remember and know," Shafer said. "I'm very proud to have grown up fishing there. Yes, Charles and I have both been very fortunate in that we've traveled, and sometimes when we're doing our best we've had very good exposure and publicity to what we're doing or have done. But when I go back home, in no way do I feel superior to the guys that have stayed there their entire lives. They're still dangerous fisherman who could beat me out on any given day."

When the proposed new museum opens at Oregon Inlet to pay tribute to the area's rich boatbuilding and sportfishing history, a visitor will have the opportunity to soak in every exhibit and then drive down to Hatteras to Ernie Foster's office that doubles as a small museum of his precious corner of the East Coast's fishing mecca. Many of the same people who visit those centers of the area's history will also book a charter, and after a day out in the deep they will realize that the stories that drew them to the Outer Banks weren't embellished in the least.

They will discover for themselves that the fishing and the boats here are exceptional, but the real treasure will come if those visitors take a little while to sit out on the docks, or at a local dining spot, to hear the stories of the captains and the mates who have poured their heart into this coastline for decades. Only then will they realize that as sleek and fast as a Carolina boat runs, and as abundant and varied as the fishing potential remains day in and day out, the real treasure of the Outer Banks is her people.

Acknowledgements

"I WOULD LIKE TO THANK EVERYONE WHO SHARED THEIR PERSONAL HISTORY AND PHOTOGRAPHS AND AGREED TO BE INTERVIEWED FOR THIS BOOK. I HOPE I'VE REMEMBERED EVERYONE."

Charles Perry

John Bayliss

Mike Bennett

Stewart Bell

Sunny Briggs

Kenneth Brown

Willie Etheridge

Ernie Foster

Dickie Harris

Buddy Hooper

Paul Mann Billy McGaskill

Mike Merritt

Bobby Scarborough

Ricky Scarborough Jr.

Chip Shafer

Paul Spencer

Sam Stokes

Homer Styron

Bobby Sullivan

Moon Tillett

Tony Tillett

Bull Tolson

Last but not least...

THIS BOOK WOULD NOT HAVE BEEN AS COMPLETE
WITHOUT THE GREAT IDEAS AND THE SKILLFUL EDITING
OF MY WONDERFUL BRIDE, JESSICA LOOSE.

HER WORK HAS MADE *BIG FISH BETTER BOATS* A BETTER BOOK.

Thank you, Jessica!

www.ingramcontent.com/pod-product-compliance
Lightning Source LLC
Chambersburg PA
CBHW070043100426

42740CB00013B/2780